NOW I
BELIEVE
YOU

REBECCA GORDON
& DARLENE KINSON

BALBOA.
PRESS

A DIVISION OF HAY HOUSE

Balboa Press books may be ordered through booksellers or by contacting:

Balboa Press
A Division of Hay House
1663 Liberty Drive
Bloomington, IN 47403
www.balboapress.com
1 (877) 407-4847

Because of the dynamic nature of the Internet, any web addresses or links contained in this book may have changed since publication and may no longer be valid. The views expressed in this work are solely those of the author and do not necessarily reflect the views of the publisher, and the publisher hereby disclaims any responsibility for them.

The author of this book does not dispense medical advice or prescribe the use of any technique as a form of treatment for physical, emotional, or medical problems without the advice of a physician, either directly or indirectly. The intent of the author is only to offer information of a general nature to help you in your quest for emotional and spiritual well-being. In the event you use any of the information in this book for yourself, which is your constitutional right, the author and the publisher assume no responsibility for your actions.

Any people depicted in stock imagery provided by Thinkstock are models, and such images are being used for illustrative purposes only.
Certain stock imagery © Thinkstock.

Print information available on the last page.

ISBN: 978-1-5043-7154-4 (sc)
ISBN: 978-1-5043-7155-1 (hc)
ISBN: 978-1-5043-7170-4 (e)

Library of Congress Control Number: 2016920637

Balboa Press rev. date: 12/13/2016

Acknowledgments

We are indebted to the following people for their patience, guidance, and support while we were busy writing our first endeavor together.

To our husbands, Jim and Tom. We thank you for putting up with all the hours spent online, on the telephone, and all the travel miles logged to get this book accomplished.

To all our friends and family who supported and encouraged us at home and on Facebook with overwhelming interest and love.

To Stacy McIntyre, professional artist, for helping Becki design and paint the cover in oils of Darlene's divine view of what she saw upon her arrival to the other side, her Nana who was sitting on the rock waiting for her.

To all our loved ones in heaven who also supported us from the other side with their divine guidance and messages, God, the Angels, Archangels, Jesus, and higher Masters—we thank you and love you unconditionally.

To Balboa Press for your guidance and support.

Live your life from your heart,
share from your heart,
and your
story will touch and heal people's souls

—Melody Beattie

INTRODUCTION

by Becki Dole Gordon

Having a near death experience (NDE) can sometimes be hard to share with others, since we find most people are resistant to believing in life after death. Our intention to share this story with you is based upon our spiritual beliefs, which have grown to nurture us throughout our lives as best friends and adults.

We want to share a bit of our history, beginning from when Darlene and I (Becki) first met as twelve-year-olds and through to this day in our late fifties, just now writing about it. It has taken us a lifetime to understand why this happened to Darlene and to see that it was meant to be a life purpose for both of us to share with others. We have learned in our hearts that there is life after death and that there is nothing to fear about it.

The idea to write this account came to me in the middle of the night after asking my guides and angels, whom I now trust and believe in fully. I awoke to thoughts of my best friend, Darlene, who was found dead but was brought back to life after a terrible car crash in 1978. She tried to explain to others and me her divine vivid experience and memories of heaven, something I had never believed in until the past twenty years or so.

My spiritual awakening and believing began in my mid-thirties when I was studying to become an occupational therapist in college and my philosophy teacher brought up the subject of God. The responses resonated with me and were so diverse and uplifting, making me question all I had learned in my own Episcopal church all my life. I began seeking to learn more. I further studied Western literature and history in college, topics I was drawn to, expanding my knowledge and explanation to other possibilities and religions that also made sense to me. I found myself becoming more aware and open-minded about near death experiences, so I felt a strong urge to write a book by the time I was in my fifties. I wanted to know more about Darlene's experience. I felt we should write this book together.

I had to tell Darlene, "Now I believe you, my friend!" Darlene wasn't receptive at first. It took a lot of convincing to get her to share her account about heaven with me because everyone, including me, had rejected her story for so long. As soon as she began writing, the memories flooded back like the events had just happened. She said it was like being there all over again, and she thanked me for badgering her to do it.

Darlene tells about her intense eight-and-a-half week recovery in the hospital after the car crash. She shares how this was very important to her spiritual awakening with vivid memories that have helped her to this day, helping her heal by writing them down in this manuscript. For many years, she tried to wrap her head around her experience in heaven without anyone to talk to who believed her. She knew, without a shadow of a doubt, that it was real. This story is from Darlene's own personal experience with the Other Side. It is totally her own account. The events did happen, and there is scientific proof today when this happens to someone, so it has to be real—as we write about later in the book! We hope that reading this book will enlighten you, the reader, with peace and comfort in knowing that we don't physically die when our lives end here; we get to go Home.

The story explains how I (Becki) came to believe her and how it has affected our lives today. We now see ourselves as mature, intelligent adults enjoying how this book has brought us much closer than ever as friends. We were just a couple of wild and crazy girls in the seventies with a great whimsical side to our personalities and the antics that we shared together. We became best friends and still are, with a lifetime of spiritual awakenings that always take us to higher realms together.

From our hearts and souls, here goes …

Chapter 1

Us Growing Up

Becki

As typical teenagers growing up in a small city in New Hampshire, and being the only girls in our families, Darlene and I were starved for female companionship. Our souls met in 1969, at the age of twelve when we were in eighth grade. We sat one seat apart and one row over from each other, and we became soul sisters by the end of that year. We were oblivious to the world, and we were full of life and ready for adventure. We grew up attending separate churches with our families, participated in Sunday school and catechism, and we knew the Bible and about Jesus and such, like our ancestors had taught us. We rebelled against going to church in our teenage years, as it sure wasn't on our minds as being fun or interesting at the time. I volunteered at our church suppers with my mom and Darlene, and I went to church on the holidays as a tradition.

We spent all our weekends together, always on a mission to have as much fun as possible, no matter how much sneaking around our parents we had to do. We vacationed together with each other's families in the summers, camping and beaching in Maine and New Hampshire. We were boy-crazy as hell and a little on the wild side, to say the least! We created and starred in our own 8mm movies using Darlene's family camera at her house. This gave us hours of entertainment, laughs, and giggles, and we were full of innocent fun. We still enjoy these movies time and again and still laugh at all the captured antics we were more than ready to perform in front of the camera.

Living life as teenage girls during the early 1970s—when smoking cigarettes and pot was considered cool and our life motto of *Got Party?* was our goal—we fully capitalized on that motto. We didn't think we were wild and crazy at the time, but looking back now, we sure were. If there were a party around, we would find it, and the parents never knew about it. We were very good at finding an excuse to get out of the house. Darlene and I were joined at the hip. We both were good cheerleaders for the Catholic Youth Organization (CYO) basketball team and our high school varsity football team. We played together on our high school's JV and varsity tennis teams, and we were both good athletes to boot. I was head cheerleader for the CYO boys' basketball team. We enjoyed each other's company immensely. We were always cheerful and willing to help others. Neither of us considered ourselves beautiful, just believing that we had average looks—but we had no trouble attracting good-looking boys! Darlene was a strawberry blond with freckles and brown eyes, and I had brown hair and blue eyes. We were both slim and five feet five inches tall, so wearing the same size shoes and clothes was convenient.

There was never a dull moment! We were always having fun and laughing our heads off. We spent our high school open lunch out on the town and would giggle so hard I would pee in my pants on a regular basis because I didn't take the time to relieve my bladder beforehand. One time during the winter, when out on lunch, we were laughing so hard at some crazy thing one of us had just said or done, and I ended up wetting my pants. My jeans froze to my legs within minutes, causing a bad rash to appear. This one particular incident sent us walking back to Darlene's house so I could change into some dry jeans. Usually, we would end up missing the afternoon session of school. (We really *hated* when that happened!) Darlene's mom couldn't get mad, as she was so humored by us—most of the time. To this day, Darlene never forgets to tell those stories when we are out with friends. I am so embarrassed, and she will never let me live that one down.

Back then, in the early '70s, the fashion style was bell-bottom hip-hugger pants, with the bells so huge that they would wrap around your ankles and trip you up when walking. Shitkicker light tan lace-up-past-your-ankle work boots, and bibbed farmer jeans overalls were all staples in every middle class student's wardrobe—or so it seemed. Everyone, boys and girls alike, wore long hair, and most of the girls wore the same perfume, *Charlie*.

Our generation of no worries—of feeling like free birds, of living in the moment, and experimenting with smoking cigarettes, pot, and drinking alcohol—was pretty much the norm, and you weren't considered cool if you didn't at least try the lifestyle. Peer pressure was high. In our later teens we were frequent visitors at the bars in Vermont even before we were the drinking age of eighteen, as we lived on the border of it and because nobody knew us there. We were never carded at the door. Many classmates and friends our age were doing the same thing, and most times our parents never knew. Things were so different back then. The laws weren't as strict. Cops took away our beer many times when we were out driving around with boys. They told us to just go home, and our parents were never called. We are not proud to admit that we drove home drunk all the time on the curvy back roads of Vermont, and I even crashed my Mother's car one time.

These are just a few experiences we shared together. We had angels watching over us, even then.

One memorable time, Darlene's dad grounded her for a month after we had jump-started my mom's car and decided to make an evening of it out with my boyfriend. Darlene was spending the night at my house on Easter Eve, 1974. We were both seventeen at the time. My boyfriend got out of work at 11:00 p.m., and that night after he called me, we went to pick him up with my mom's car. We certainly made a night of it!

I surrendered the driving to my boyfriend for the rest of the night. Our first stop was at the local store for a case of beer, then on to a house on the other side of town for a pound of weed. Our final leg of the night found us out on dirt back roads that surrounded our little town. We missed a left-hand turn, and so naturally the car was slapped into reverse and gunned. We came to a very sudden and abrupt halt. We had backed into a telephone pole at breakneck speed, causing a perfectly-shaped butt crack in the rear of my mom's car!

The three of us then continued onward, going down yet another dirt road to find ourselves watching two best friends, starters on our CYO boys' basketball team, slugging it out in the headlights of their parked car. The fight ended, they climbed in, and we all continued to party. As we were heading home, we wound up completely sideways in a ditch. We were not stuck, but we were racing along the ditch watching the dirt rush past us from the car door windows. Yep ... the paint was completely gone the whole length of that side of my mom's car. It was at this time that I decided my boyfriend needed to go home—and so did we—as the skies were starting to lighten. When we got to my house, Darlene and I opted to push my mom's car backward into the garage. This way my mom wouldn't see the naked side of her car right off. (Like that was going to make a difference.)

Mom and my little brother were planning on going to Sunrise Service at Mom's church. Just as we sneaked into the living room and assumed our positions in bed, Mom's alarm went off and church prep was in gear. Whew! That was close! Darlene and I snuggled down deeper into our covers to look like we were in a deep sleep. Mom and my little brother were trying to be quiet and not wake us up. My little brother went out to the garage to get into the car, and he spied the naked side of the car. He ran inside, yelling for my mom, and she followed him out to the garage. Within seconds, we heard the first scream of disbelief, soon to be followed by a second scream as she discovered the new butt crack on the back of her car.

My full name was erupting from Mom's mouth as she came bursting into the living room, grabbed the cot where Darlene was lying, and flung it over. Darlene was on the floor as my mom continued to scream and yell while punching, hitting, and kicking her. Mom thought I was one on the cot. When Mom realized it was Darlene she was beating the hell out of, she just yelled, "Well, you deserve it too!" Darlene's parents were called, and her Dad was not pleased at all. Darlene had to pay my mother $1,300 for her share of the expense of Mom's car to be fixed. We were separated for more than a month. I felt pretty bad. We were so upset, and a lesson was kind of learned.

My mom was easygoing and allowed me a lot of freedom. She was raising my brother, who was ten years younger, and she worked a lot of overtime as a secretary to support us. Therefore, she didn't have time for my issues as a teenager. My parents were divorced, so my strict dad wasn't around, and I got away with everything. Poor Darlene got the punishment every time. We were always getting caught with boys at places we weren't supposed to be, mostly skipping out of the dances to go drinking in old St. Mary's cemetery. When we skipped school we would show up to party at Darlene's brother's house, which was only walking distance away from the high school.

Darlene often spoke of her intuition and was able to predict our destiny—things that happened to us that she already knew were coming. She knew when her dad was after us, when I thought we were perfectly safe, and sure enough he was right there! She would also hear and see things, so I thought she was crazy for sure. I never believed her when she would say odd things, like when she would say she saw her grandmother or another person who had passed come to visit her. I thought she was dreaming or making it up. I would hear it but would ignore it, thinking it was a figment of her imagination.

Any chance to party in those days was the goal. We were not bad girls; we just liked to have fun and were willing to take risks to do so. It was worth getting in trouble for, I guess. My mother always wrote absence notes for me and Darlene, so we didn't get into trouble for missing school. She was so easy; I'm lucky I turned out okay! My grades surely showed it. They were terrible, except for English class, which I loved. I loved writing even then. We weren't going to church anymore at that age, as it wasn't important to us, and our parents had given up trying to make us go.

We never missed our CYO dances with Aerosmith and other great bands playing, paying only one dollar to get in and they would play from 8 p.m. to 12 a.m. (Who would have known the local boys from our area would be so famous one day?) The boyfriends were coming and going like the wind. Usually we would take off in a car with boys, drinking during the dances and sometimes getting caught by Darlene's dad. He caught on to us when we got a little older. The duo of trouble! We didn't make the popular clique in school. We liked it better that way. We could be ourselves.

There were a couple of weekend trips we took with the CYO called the *Search*. Darlene explains it more in another chapter, but that was a little window of spiritual awakening for both of us when we realized there was something more than just church in the spirit world. We came back from these weekends different teenagers, with a high on life that eventually would wear off. We never forgot sharing that experience together, and we talk about it to this day.

We still cheriesh memories of lying in the front seat of my mother's car on vacation at the Sea Latch Motel in York Beach, Maine. My mom loved to take Darlene, my little brother, and me to the ocean for two weeks each year, where we would laugh and giggle for hours. This was a highlight of our lives. After a long day on the beach, biking, and swimming in the pool, we would recline on the front seats back of Mom's Toyota, listening to the Beatles' *Sgt. Pepper's Lonely Hearts Club Band* album with our favorite song "A Day in the Life" blasting from the eight-track player. We would sing our lungs out for the entire album and then play it over and over again for hours. We had my mom's car just a-rocking during those hours of listening pleasure. Those were the good ol' days! We had much more freedom than kids do today. (We turned out just fine, by the way.)

We both had jobs during and after graduating high school in 1975. I worked at the local grocery store for $3.25 an hour, which wasn't too bad a salary at that time. Darlene had already secured a job at McDonald's her sophomore year of high school at the age of fifteen, (due to her father's insistence that you learn to "make your way as soon as possible"). We moved in together for a short time after high school, and that was an experience. Even as best friends, we had our differences. For example, she was a clean freak, and I wasn't! We always had a house full of animals. Soon our interests separated us. I went off to Florida for two years to earn an associate's degree in business management in Fort Lauderdale. I felt the need to make a big change and see the world a bit, and I took a big scary step all by myself. It was more fun than studying but I did graduate. Darlene continued to work at McDonald's, keeping in touch by letters, infrequent phone calls, and when I came home for visits.

In May of 1978, just as I graduated from college and came home from Florida, Darlene had thought she found her soul mate, Tom. He was a tall, dark- haired, handsome guy who seemed nice enough to me. She and Tom were into partying, drinking, smoking pot, and were also doing other drugs of choice for entertainment, as most our age group was doing in the late '70s. I got most of the partying out of my system in Fort Lauderdale while attending college and was ready to settle down at home by that time. I found a bunch of friends I'd just met since coming home and took a new job at a manufacturing company in payroll. My mom had worked there for thirty-five years and got me the job, and it paid pretty well. I hadn't seen much of Darlene. She was running with a crowd of people I didn't know and was into the partying lifestyle hardcore. She was smoking a lot of pot and using cocaine and speed on a daily basis. We drifted apart. I met a tall, dark, and handsome boyfriend at work who was older, and I had a new life with my new friends. Parties were still on the agenda on the weekends—disco dancing to Donna Summer, the Bee Gees, and KC and the Sunshine Band, just to name a few bands that were popular at the local bar/restaurant in town. My new friends gathered three nights a week to socialize and dance. We had great times, dressing up in high heels and dresses. I had my own apartment, and life was good.

Darlene and I were still besties though, no matter what. We talked at least once a week, and then our lives changed with a *bang!* In late May of 1978 right after Memorial Day, I received a phone call from our mutual friend, Donnalee, who had also been very close with us in high school. She's the one who told me the sad news that Darlene and Tom had been in a very bad accident and that they didn't think she was going to make it. We would never forget this day for the rest of our lives. The shock of hearing news of my best friend being in a possible fatal car accident put me in a state of absolute disbelief. How could this be?

She was in a coma, had IVs and tubes running into and all over her body, was intubated to breath, and had three closed head injuries—grim, to say the least. She was being kept alive by a ventilator, and her parents were receiving half-hourly reports of her condition for the first three days. I was in shock and disbelief. I thought she was going to die, not knowing she already had and had come back. My heart was empty, and I prayed so hard. I hadn't been very spiritual or close to God over the past several years, but I needed him now, I knew. I wasn't allowed at the hospital to see her because she was in intensive care. I wanted to go so badly! I called her mom and dad as soon as I received the news, and they told me what they knew. Her Parents were beside themselves with grief and were terrified by the thought of losing their daughter. She suffered several broken ribs, and two of these ribs were broken, so if she moved around at all they would spear one of her lungs and she would most likely suffocate and die. She had extensive lung damage due to drowning, major head trauma, and was in a coma. It didn't look good. All I could do was pray for God to save her. It was at least two weeks before anyone other than family could see her. I couldn't see her for almost a month after the accident. When she was finally out of the intensive care unit and moved to another room, I was able to visit her for the first time. It was truly a miracle that she survived.

She was so skinny and could hardly talk, and she had a very raspy voice from all the dirt and grit that she had breathed in from the bottom of the brook. She was intubated for the entire time she was in intensive care, with tubes and IVs going in and out everywhere, and she couldn't walk. I just couldn't believe it. I have to say that experience made us closer. She recovered but will always have a raspy voice, and her lungs will never be the same. I would always hear her making remarks about what she had seen in heaven, but she didn't really come out and tell me the whole thing. She knew I wasn't going to believe her. And she was right! For many years after that, I thought it was just a dream or the heavy medication she was on during her first hours and days in the hospital—until I woke up spiritually.

Chapter 2

NOBODY BELIEVED ME

Darlene

Many times throughout my life, I had experienced a deep *knowing* about things, places, and people but never knew I was in the spiritual realm. These things would just happen. The few times I would broach the subject, it was either rejected by the person I was speaking with, or they told me it was my imagination. It was as if I had to bear this burden alone. It *was* a burden. I am now, in my late fifties, beginning to understand that this is a gift. It's not always a pleasant experience, and there are many times I don't understand why these things are coming to me. What am I supposed to do with them?

It's like the spirits of people who have passed from life to death were—and still are—trying to send messages through me, but for whom? This is truly a gift, I know, but I wish I knew how to use it more to the advantage of helping people.

My nana, who was on my mother's side, died on Monday, November 15, 1971. I was a freshman in high school and fourteen years old. I was devastated. I remember one day close to the first-year anniversary date of Nana's death, I had started my sophomore year in high school, and my day had been a very difficult one. I was in my bedroom when a vision came. There was a small two-seat sofa that had been part of my parents' very first living room set when they were married, and it was in my room across from my bed. Behind it was one of my bedroom windows facing west. Mom and Dad hadn't gotten home from work yet. I was lying on my bed facing the sofa and was in the throes of an emotional hissy fit. I noticed that at the end of the sofa that was nearest to me, a small cloud of what looked like dust began to swirl around on the bottom edge of the side of the couch, and then *poof!* Nana appeared on the sofa! She was in a dazzling white gown, and the late afternoon sun was coming in through the window behind the sofa. The light from the window made it look like Nana's red hair was a glorious crown of red around her head. I wasn't sure if I was really seeing this or if I was losing my faculties. Nana sat with her arm draped over the armrest of the sofa and just looked at me. I finally realized that it was her, and I bolted upright on my bed. I'm positive my mouth hung open like a broken gate, and I stared at her in disbelief and awe. She asked me what the trouble was. I related my difficult day to her. Nana's face was soft with compassion, and she told me that this difficult time of missing her would pass, and I'd be stronger from it.

Things are not a coincidence; they are part of *the plan*. To be truthful, I didn't get it then. What plan? Strong *how?* What did this mean? Before I could ask these questions, she blew an air kiss and was gone. However, her essence lingered in my bedroom for quite awhile. This was the first time after her funeral I had seen her spirit clearly.

When I was very young, four or five years old, my mother and I would visit Nana at her house in her little hometown in New Hampshire. On more than just a couple of occasions, I saw this tall, scruffy-looking man. He was dressed in dirty farmer overalls, a dirty white T-shirt, and wore muckers on his feet that would be covered in mud. He stood in the doorway to the small bedroom off the living room that was once my favorite aunt's bedroom. Normally, he wouldn't move or say anything; he would just stand there watching me. At first I thought he was just another person who Nana and Grandpa were letting live there for a short time.

My grandparents were always opening up their house to people who were down on their luck, giving them a warm bed, three meals a day, and a hand up. So, when I saw him, I wouldn't freak out. But this one time, he *did* move. He reached around the back of him and grabbed a red handkerchief from his back pocket and wiped his face. I said, "Hello." No response. "Hello," I said again. No response. He turned and disappeared into the bedroom. I went to the doorway and looked inside, but he wasn't anywhere to be seen. Now, this freaked me out! I ran into the kitchen and told Nana and my mother what I had just seen. Nana asked me to describe him to her. When I did, she had a shocked and concerned look on her face. Apparently, when my grandparents had purchased this property, the man I saw on this occasion was the previous owner and ran an illegal drug ring for quite some time from this house. The business posed as a vegetable stand at the base of the long, sloping upward driveway to the house. He died a violent death at the foot of the driveway. Nana had a Catholic priest come and exorcise the house. I never saw that man there again.

There were other times when, as a young child, I would get these feelings. I had feelings like dread, fear, or the sensation that I was not supposed to be where I was at that moment. I didn't know what to do with these feelings. I couldn't explain them to anyone. I would just react and remove myself from the situation. What happened when I experienced this, most times, was that someone I was with would get hurt—not in a life-threatening way, but injured just the same. That, along with the feeling, would upset me. I began to feel that I was the cause of other people's bad luck. I felt alone and jinxed.

The summer of 1965, my dad had managed to secure a good paying job at a trucking company in Vermont. The job he had at the shoe shop in our town in New Hampshire was not doing so well. He had to secure odd jobs just to feed and clothe us three kids. Mom was able to lace shoes for the same shoe shop awhile, but that too had stopped because of the economic downslide of the shoe shop. So we moved to another small town in New Hampshire, which was just on the other side of the Connecticut River. I was going into the third grade, and we were an hour- and-a-half away from our first home in New Hampshire and my nana.

Mom was a stay-at-home mom. Even though it was a small town, there were plenty of kids in our neighborhood for us to play with. My dad's older sister and her family lived just up around the corner from us. It was a nice place to be, only Nana was so far away.

Our closest neighbors had five children. We were all pretty much the same age and became close friends. The two and a half years we were there have always been my fondest memories. We would gather at the neighbors for almost everything! Their living room was where I first saw "It's the Great Pumpkin, Charlie Brown," the Halloween cartoon. It was a treat! They had a color TV! On occasion, my mom, we three kids, and the neighbors' brood of five would climb Fall Mountain that sloped up from behind my aunt's house. We'd eventually end up at Table Rock that gave us a panoramic view of the valley below.

My intuitions were always with me. When a neighborhood classmate of mine severed his Achilles tendon while we were all playing hide-and-seek in their backyard, I knew he was going to get hurt. I didn't tell him. I felt so responsible for his injury, and it was hard to look him in the face. He was my classmate, a good friend, and I allowed him to get hurt. I didn't warn him. I felt so bad. The ever- present question of *will he believe me?* prevented me from saying anything to him.

Having a special birthday date, of sorts, and birthday parties with tons of friends in attendance were things I never really had as a young child, because my birthday falls just seven days before Christmas. The first time we planned a birthday party for me, I was in the first grade. It was supposed to begin after school got out that day. However, that day started out cold, dark, and very cloudy. You could smell the snow in the air. Yup! We got snow that day. After school was let out for the day, my older brother and I trudged up the steep hill to our house to find Mom out in the driveway with shovel in hand. She was almost done clearing the fluffy snow from the driveway. She told us to go inside to get ready for my party, and we did just that. I was *so* excited! I changed from my school clothes into my frilly Easter dress and patent leather shoes (both of which were worn only for special occasions) and took my place at the head of the table in the *special girl* chair Nana had decorated just for me. It faced the kitchen door. I knew my classmates would start arriving soon.

Mom and Nana had gone all out for this. Matching pink and blue paper plates, cups, tablecloth, and napkins, noisemakers, birthday hats, and my big chocolate cake with chocolate frosting adorned the kitchen table that had been transformed from *everyday* into *magical.* I was seated, patiently waiting for my classmates to arrive. I was looking out the kitchen window at the thick blanket of snow now falling and covering the outside with fluffy, white crystals. I waited, and the phone rang. I continued waiting. The phone rang again. I waited longer. For the next few minutes the phone did not stop ringing. The snow continued to fall outside. I was still waiting. Eventually, Mom had to break the bad news. No one was coming. The snowstorm was too much for anyone to make it through. I was sitting in my *special girl* chair, staring at the dense, unrelenting, blanket of snow now claiming the outdoors, and I started to sob. It was my birthday!

Grandpa arrived in the driveway, and the snow that Mom had cleared out earlier was practically up to his knees. He trudged into the house with the chocolate ice cream Nana had sent him for. He glanced around, and the look on his face showed that he knew no one had made it to my party. Grandpa, Howard Bixby Sr., reached for me and gave me a big bear hug. He was saying something, but I didn't hear it. The utter letdown of this event was all-consuming. Nana, Mildred Bixby, and Grandpa left but not before Nana enveloped me in her arms. She had tears in her eyes. Nana leaned down to hug me and give me my birthday kiss, and my grandparents headed for home. They had a tricky five-mile drive back to their farmhouse. Mom didn't know what to do. She tried to comfort me, but I was inconsolable. She let me be. I still sat in my chair and prayed that the snow would stop and that I would still have my party! The gray daylight faded into darkness outside the window. Mom started supper. *Dad should be home from work soon,* I thought. Car lights came up the driveway, and Dad came home from work. He trudged through the snow into the kitchen. He shook the snow off his coat and boots. He looked at the table still adorned with my party settings and looked at Mom, who gave a little shake of her head, *no.* Dad looked back at me and came over to me. He lifted me out of "my" chair and hugged me. He was so sorry! The dam broke, and I buried my head into his strong shoulder and cried like I had never cried before. Mom said, "We can have our own special party." She suggested I could still sit in my chair and Dad could sit in the other chair. That was the only party I had ever planned. After that, I didn't want to plan on having birthday parties—*ever!*

In the fall of 1967, Dad had secured a better paying job in Vermont, at a machine shop. The little house we were renting was beginning to be too small for our parents and three growing kids. Dad wanted to buy a house. So, the quest began. One Sunday afternoon, we all piled into the car to go north to look at houses, to a larger city that was twenty-two miles north of where we were in New Hampshire. We looked at several that day. The last place we looked at was an apartment house. It was a split-level two-apartment building. The owner had just passed away, and the house was in need of much TLC. Perfect! My Dad loved to putter, and he was good at painting, wallpapering, laying floors, and so on. The yard was huge! Dad bought the apartment house that would fit our size family. One early sunny, fall Saturday, we packed our belongings into the moving truck with the help of a couple of neighbors trucks, and we were gone. It was a very bittersweet moment in my life.

I had loved being in my old little town. I had never had a shortage of friends to hang out with. I didn't feel good about this move. Being in fifth grade now, I was pretty much established with the kids from back home. This was scary. Mom and Dad enrolled us in St. Mary's Catholic School. I knew on the first day of school that this was not going to be a good experience. Very few of the kids attempted to be friendly with me. I was stared at and snickered at and made to feel the outcast. I felt so alone. I knew I was "different" from these kids, and it was difficult to adapt. I turned inward on myself. I became awkward, unsure, and afraid. My intuition about things that were about to happen—or feeling like I knew all about a place I had never been—continued to haunt me. I didn't *know* anyone there. It was a long time before I felt safe enough to be sociable. I longed to be back with my friends in my old hometown.

I attended St. Mary's Catholic school until I finished seventh grade. I wanted to go to public school. I didn't have any close friends at St. Mary's, and I was the odd duck out. It took me several pleas to convince my parents that I could handle public school better than Catholic school. The fact that I didn't have many friends seemed to cinch the deal. So, in the fall of 1969 I started eighth grade at the junior high. It was a breath of fresh air. So many different kids! Such a big school! I had a lot of opportunities to challenge myself. It was here that I let my guard down on my intuition and began to feel "normal." I was in Mrs. B.'s homeroom. There was a pretty girl in the row next to me who seemed a bit shy. She had beautiful brown hair that fell just past her shoulders. She wore the coolest clothes. I wanted to meet her. I don't recall how our friendship began exactly, but within weeks Becki and I were fast friends. Finally—I had a friend! I didn't realize it then, but we were destined to be in each other's lives for a lifetime.

Becki and I were pretty much two peas in a pod. Looking back now, I realize that I never really came out and told her about my intuitions. I'd smooth them over with my own doubt. How would she react if I told her about these feelings I'd get when things were happening? How would this information affect our friendship? She'd think I was nuts! So I kept them to myself. I felt terribly conflicted. I was beginning to doubt their validity myself. I excelled on the community swim team. That was my outlet. Once I was in high school, I stopped the swim team. My interest in tennis, cheerleading, gymnastics, and Outward Bound took up all my free time. For my fifteenth birthday, my parents bought me a French ten-speed racing bike. It was awesome! Becki and I once actually biked the twenty-two miles south to my old hometown, and that little jaunt took us the entire day. I took her around my old neighborhood. I showed her the school, the Catholic church, the place I first sneaked a sip of beer from my uncle's stolen beer bottle, and the little house I loved so much.

I think what I loved the most about that little house was the fireplace. During the holidays, the space between the fireplace and the dining area window was where the Holy Grail of Christmas stood. We bought our first artificial Christmas tree the second year we were there. Lots of smiles and giggles happened around that tree. It was always magical for me to visit this little hamlet of my youth. Most of my old haunts were still there, but it had all changed so much too. The neighbors had moved away. The kids I remembered were all scattered about living in different houses or had moved away. The only constant was my aunt and her family, who were still living in their house at the foot of the Fall Mountain.

After high school, Becki went off to Fort Lauderdale in Florida for college and left me behind. We didn't stay in close contact, but whenever she came home for a visit, we would reunite, and the time of separation was evaporated. We were two peas in a pod again. Time to party! (And party we did.)

Becki returned to college, and my new boyfriend Tom and I moved to a different apartment over a local market. I worked nights as a cocktail waitress at the popular local restaurant/bar.

It was a beautiful spring day, and the strangest thing happened. I was standing at my kitchen sink doing the morning dishes. Tom left to go to the grocery store and had the day off from his job. He had just left the apartment, and my hands were fluffing the dish soap in the sink readying for the task of washing them. All of a sudden, the air in my bright, sunny kitchen seemed too thin, making it hard to breathe. The air was filled with the stench of sulfur and diseased, rotting flesh. I had the sense that someone was standing behind me. I knew no one else was there because only Tom and I lived there. The hair at the base of my neck stood up straight. I felt as if I were suffocating and began to feel panic rising in my chest. What was going on?

Suddenly, the walls were closing in, and the atmosphere in the kitchen turned dank and oppressive. I *felt* rather than *saw* the air thickening. I didn't want to turn around. I could hear a raspy inhaling of oxygen behind me. I spun around. What I saw standing menacingly in the middle of my kitchen made me gasp in horror. I didn't believe what I saw. The figure looked exactly like what I had perceived in my mind of Satan himself. He was at least eight feet tall and was hunched over at the waist, because he was taller than my kitchen ceiling. There were swirling mists of a smelly stench revolving around his cloaked head. He was clad in a long, black hooded robe that hung over the top of his head, so as not to show his whole face. I could only see his red eyes and yellow, stained teeth. He didn't say anything at first. He just stood there clutching the neck of his black robe, glaring at me and breathing heavily. I'm sure my eyes were bugging out of my head, and my mouth was probably open. I was terrified!

When I felt like I was about to drop unconscious, he began to laugh. At first it was a slow rumbling in his chest, but then it erupted into the most horrific sound I had ever heard—before or since. His huge head reared, and swirls of a more foul-smelling stench escaped into the already stinking air as he laughed at me. His head dropped back to his chest, and he leveled his eyes at me. All appearance of mirth was gone. Only hatred radiated from him through his bloodshot eyes, which were now trained on me. I knew I was going to faint. I don't know why I didn't. He raised his left arm toward me and stuck out his gnarled, grotesquely misshaped index finger, and hissed, "I own you! You will never escape me!" I was frozen in terror. Why was he here? What was happening? And with that, he was gone. The foul stench he left behind was in our apartment for the next few days.

Later that night, Tom came to the restaurant while I was working. His face was ashen and his hands were trembling. He sat at the bar and drank four draft beers one right after the other. I approached him and was very concerned. He had never acted like that before. Between running drink orders to other patrons in the bar, I asked him several times what was wrong—and he finally told me. While he was sitting in our living room watching television, he had seen dozens of little demon-looking creatures coming out of the closet to the right of where the TV sat. They carried sharp spear-type things in their hands and were jabbing him in the legs, while sadistically laughing at him, screaming at him, and dancing around his chair. At this point, he rolled up his pant legs, and on both of his calves were slashes that were bleeding a bit. I had not told him about the experience I'd had just hours before in the kitchen. I had thought that I was hallucinating from the drugs I was constantly doing, and I certainly didn't expect Tom would have his own terrifying experience. This was only a couple of days before the crash. Maybe this was a warning, and we were unaware of what was to come. We have yet to figure that out, even though the hideous beings would be appearing in my future experience.

Chapter 3

MEMORIAL DAY, MAY 28, 1978
THE CRASH

Darlene

Wow! That's a bad car accident! I thought as I looked upon a small car that hung precariously on the stream embankment. The car was a four-door yellow 1976 Fiat. It sat half in and half out of the small stream that flowed around a bend and under the road. The front end of the car was smashed in, and the back window was missing. The condition of the car reminded me of a handful of aluminum foil crumpled into a ball and ready to be thrown away. I said to myself, *I hope everyone is okay.*

From the perch where I was sitting, I noticed two young men. One was lying near the rear of the car on the furthest embankment of the stream and was in the throes of hysterical laughter. *Why is he laughing?* I thought. It was an unnatural sound for someone to be laughing in the aftermath of a horrific car accident. It seemed to me that he was completely out of control. I found out later that he was in the middle of a diabetic seizure and that he always laughed uncontrollably when experiencing one of them. The other young man was frantically darting in and out of the stream yelling, "My baby! My baby!" He'd lost his baby! Watching this nightmarish scenario unfold before my eyes, all I could think was, *This is not going to turn out well!*

There was an odd sense that I knew these two young men, but who were they? Where had I met them? How did I know them? What were their names? I couldn't recall.

I couldn't watch anymore. I looked away. Immediately, I had the sensation of leaving this scene and ascending upward at a very high rate of speed. I also recall that I was not alone. A presence—not hostile, not angry, and not intimidating—was my travel companion. The feeling of not being alone was oddly comforting. *What is happening?* I wondered. *And why?* I didn't know the answer to those two questions. So, I just sat back and enjoyed the ride. The wind that was blowing through my hair and over my face was quite turbulent, but I had no problem breathing. I glanced around. To the left, right, front, up, and down from me was the color blue. Not Crayola blue but presently blue, and by that I mean it is always blue at any given moment. I just wasn't sure if it would stay that particular shade of present, perfect blue or if it would change to a different hue. Incredible! Never before—or since—have I seen this shade of blue. However, I was not permitted to look backward over my shoulder to see my guide. My head would turn to a point, and then it would be turned back to the front by an unseen hand. The touch was not hostile, but it was firm and no-nonsense, like having to keep to a schedule and no monkey business tolerated. *All righty then,* I thought. *Fly on!*

Traveling at this rate of speed and feeling completely free, I realized that I was crouched in the fetal position in a huge baseball-mitt-feeling cocoon type of thing and that I was feeling absolutely safe. *Huh?* We were still at an incline on our trip. There was a definite downshift in our jet-like travel of speed, and we were now at a steeper rate of incline. Thin, misty clouds made my cheeks moist as we neared the apex of the incline. We hit a speed bump, and there was an immediate sense of being in landing mode on our journey. It was absolutely and completely exhilarating. We descended through the thin, white, moist clouds, and my vision cleared as we flew a few feet above the most beautiful meadow. I saw the grasses ruffling in the wake of our passing over them. Our landing mode was slowing us down. I noticed rabbits, squirrels, dogs, fawns, and butterflies frolicking in the waves of grass. They were running with us! They made graceful leaps in and out of the waves of ruffling grasses. It was like a welcome committee! *Welcome* seemed to emanate from this frolicking group. Our rate of travel slowed down almost to a stop. The guide of our trip efficiently deposited me into the waist-high grass and departed. I still didn't get a glimpse of the guide.

The grass was so soft against my skin. It began to settle from being ruffled by our arrival, and wasn't waist high; it was knee high. Although I didn't see the animals gathered at my feet, they did stay just out of sight in the grass. A golden or silver glint of the light nearby caught my attention, and soft brown or blue eyes of all shades looked at me from the security of the grasses covering them. I stood and looked—really looked—at my surroundings. It was very familiar yet strange at the same time. Green grass, brown dirt, yellow butterflies … everything was familiar but strange too. It was all so clear, with crystal like glinting in the golden-hued light radiating to everything, everywhere *Okay! Where am I and why am I here?* I wondered.

There were gentle, tufting breezes moving over the meadow. The grasses, flowers, and butterflies were dancing all around me. Everything moved and was making its own music. It was simply amazing! As I stood in this very large, very green, very bright, and very beautiful picturesque meadow, I was awed by the harmony of everything. Everything seemed to dance for joy. Absolute joy, peace, and love radiated from all things. Love was the prominent feeling. This was not a feeling I'd experienced before just from standing in a meadow. This was an all-encompassing feeling. Yes, I had been an outdoorsy sort of person before this, but what I witnessed and felt was complete unity with my surroundings.

This around me was tangible. This was real. This was *it*.

The breeze felt like gentle caresses. It moved over, around, and through all things. All the plant life responded in a beautiful, haunting, peaceful song. The grasses added high-pitched sing-songy sounds. The flowers contributed delicate soft swishing notes, the shrubs made a tenor-like trumpeting chorus, and the lush, full trees completed the melody with their own baritone addition. Each was awesome in its own right, but when all were combined it was simply amazing! True perfection. I had never attended a symphony orchestra concert in person, but I had watched the Boston Pops perform on TV during Christmastime. To be sure, it was wonderful, but *this* was so much more. It was truly inspiring in every sense of the word. The melodious strains that came from the botany around me were so pure, so clear, and so individually complete. I felt like I was witnessing worship in absolute harmony. This perfect blend of joy brought tears to my eyes. Where was I?

I was held in awe by the purity, clarity, and innocence of the light that illuminated this place. *Absolute love* were the words that sprang to my mind. I had never before in my life experienced this sense of utter completeness and acceptance. Yes, my parents, brothers, aunts, uncles, cousins, and grandparents were very much a part of my life, and I knew they all loved me, but this was totally and unconditionally *love* in its simplest form. More tears. I don't know how long I stood there savoring this specialness of being here.

It brought to mind the time I had gone on a "search" weekend through our CYO group in 1974 with Becki. That weekend, we had an experience that enlightened our spirits. It was a high for us like neither one of us had ever experienced. The search's purpose was to give teenagers a glimpe of the pure, positive energy of God. It was a weekend to meet other teens and be involved in guided meditation of a unique kind that I had never encountered before. The intent was to awaken the youth in attendance at the search weekend to their inner selves. We met new kids from all over the state of New Hampshire. It was a great experience! What stands out most in my mind about that weekend was when we all met in the chapel on our last night. The portable pews had been taken out of the chapel, and Sister Louise, our overseer for the weekend, had all of us sit in a large circle on the floor. Candles were lit on the altar and at various places around the chapel. The lights were then turned off, and we sat there in candlelight. I remember thinking this was a whole new sensation for me. Sister Louise took us on a journey through our creation with her soft voice. First, we were free spirits in a completely spiritual realm, experiencing the deliciousness of just *being*. In my mind's eye, I could see the billions of planets that make up the universe. I could feel the freedom and exhilaration of flowing with the energy that creates worlds. Then we were babes in our mothers' wombs. She painted a complete world of our well-being there. As Sister Louise spoke in her soft, reassuring voice, I began to feel buoyant, like I was in the fetal position. As she continued her voice painting with us, an expansion of our minds and souls was beginning to take place. It was glorious for all! I'm not sure how long we were in that little chapel soaring with our spiritual wings, but the time we spent there was not nearly long enough for me. It was a renewing of my life, my attitude, and my spirit! Becki felt the same way. I was not the same teenager then as when I first got there. It greatly changed my way of thinking about my own life.

Standing in this beautiful meadow and living this all-consuming love, the search experience waned considerably by comparison. No coaxing of this emotion … it *was*. It *is*. It was forever, eternity, past, present, and future. All of my mental, emotional, and spiritual senses recognized this presence of being all at once, no doubt. Peace. Amen.

Unexplainable waves of energy, strength, and love were poured into me, on me, and through me to overflowing. I *felt* whole and complete. I was in awe and stunned. I couldn't—more like didn't want to—move. I wanted these energies to be part of me with every fiber of my being. Forever. Cleansing. Pure. Love. I finally forced myself to open my eyes and was surprised to see that the neck and front of my T-shirt were wet. I must have been standing there with my eyes closed and crying while this total immersion of love encompassed me. I thought it odd that I was crying. Didn't being loved mean being happy? Wouldn't I be laughing, smiling, and giddy? Why was I crying? As I stood there, I knew I didn't want to move, to cause this complete love to cease coursing over me. It reminded me of how excited, eager, and full of wonder I had felt as a youngster sitting on the floor in front of our Christmas tree, waiting to open the presents that were there, and all their colorful wrappings, with my name on them, and to enjoy them as mine! Sheer joy made me tingle from head to toe. Sometimes I would actually cry from the sheer happiness of it all. Still, I stood, not wanting this experience to end. I closed my eyes again.

I opened my eyes once more. It was time to start searching for someone, anyone I could ask: "Where am I?" My quest began in earnest. As I looked around the meadow, I saw a large rock in front of me, about a football field's distance away. I began my journey toward the rock. There was someone atop the rock. *Woohoo! Another human being!* For some reason, I didn't rush. I guess I felt there was no need to. As I was walking, another oddity was present. From where I had just stepped and lifted my feet, the trampled grass plumped itself back to its previous state and arched gracefully to standing, with audible music coming from it. Butterflies were everywhere, and some fluttered around me. They seemed to assist the trodden grasses with their plumping using the beat of their wings. Amazing—nature in harmony with all things!

The distance between me and the rock became shorter very quickly. I was having so much fun dancing and running among the flowers and other plants in the field while watching them become upright again that I was surprised to see the rock was now only a few feet in front of me. The person atop of the rock—whom I noted had a female stature—was still sitting there, her back facing me. Great—another woman! She possessed a glorious crown of flaming red hair. Wait a minute. Could this have been who I thought it was? She resembled my Nana who had died several years earlier to breast cancer. Still, was that her sitting there? Standing at the foot of this rock and not believing what I think I saw, I did the only thing I could think of to get this woman's attention. I coughed an *ahem*. I must have startled her, because she turned her head around so quickly to look at me I thought she might lose her balance and topple off the rock and get hurt. She looked at me over her right shoulder and exclaimed, "Darlene! I wasn't expecting you to come in that way! I thought you'd be coming in this way!" She pointed away from me. "Well, never mind." and with that, she executed a graceful leap up into the air away from the top of the rock and came to rest face-to-face in front of me. Yup! *Nana!* The hugs and kisses I got! All the while she was hugging me and kissing my face. "Oh! I'm *so* happy to see you!" she told me. "I've missed you *so* much! My, how you've grown into a beautiful woman!" On and on she went—ya know, all the things nanas say to you since the last time they saw you.

I'm positive that my mouth was agape and that my eyes were popping out of my head. *Nana! It can't be! I'm having a very real dream!* The only thought running through my head was *Wake up!* The reality was that I was very much awake.

Eventually, Nana stood back, smiling with the most dazzling smile I'd ever seen on her face. She looked into my eyes with her crystal-clear blue eyes and asked, "What's wrong?" I could not wrap my head around this. Nana was standing before me. I could see her, I could touch her, I could hear her, and I could smell her. This just couldn't be! I was seeing her, touching her, smelling her, and still trying to grasp this situation when she asked me again, "What's wrong?" This time I blinked my eyes and gave my head a little shake. My eyes refocused and saw that Nana was physically flawless. She'd always been my beautiful Nana, flaws and all, but now she was perfect in all senses of the word. The physical flaws were no more. She was radiant! Her blue eyes were the color of a mountain lake in mid-summer, and her nose was no longer crooked from being broken the many times it had been while she grew up on a farm. (Evidently, broken noses were a "work hazard" and tended to occur on a regular basis in the early 1910s while tending to jittery livestock in the barn.)

Gone from her face were the deeply etched lines and wrinkles that had come from living and working hard and tirelessly just to survive another day on the farm during the Great Depression of 1932. She had to deal with the everyday pressures of caring for a growing family. Nana not only took care of her own family of three daughters, one son, and her husband but also took in and cared for two young nephews, one infant niece, and her brother after his wife suddenly passed away. Under Nana's care, her niece was very ill and passed away shortly after their arrival at Nana's house. So sad. Nana's voice sounded the same except that it no longer held the raspiness of years of smoking. Her voice flowed over me smooth as silk. I mustered all my energy and choked out in a whisper, "*Nana?* You're dead!" At the same time, I was struggling not to faint. I pointed my index finger into my chest and said, "I'm—" Nana put her right hand up like a police officer halting traffic, and said, "We have plenty of time for that later."

She continued her scrutiny of me and still held my face in her hands, still cooing at me like nanas do. She stepped a half-step back and said, "You look awfully thin." Well, yes, I was. I had not been living a healthy lifestyle. I had a $120-a-day cocaine and speed habit, I drank *way* too much alcohol, and I had also smoked cigarettes and pot on a daily basis for months before the accident. My general health was shaky at best. If I ate a single full meal in two days time, it was a miracle. I could only stand there and watch her watching me. I was awestruck that Nana was standing in front of me, the new and perfected version of Nana. Her attention on me was like warm bath water—comforting, relaxing, and refreshing. To actually be in her presence, to see her face, to hear her voice, and to touch her again made me feel indescribable joy. The sheer happiness I felt was, well, awesome!

When Nana had passed away, I felt betrayed, ever so alone, and so lost. I remember sitting in the Catholic church in my birth town in New Hampshire for her funeral services. I wasn't listening to the service. I sat in the pew and just stared at her coffin. Nana was really gone! I was sitting between my mom and her older sister, my aunt. I looked away from Nana's coffin and was staring at the crucifix that hung on the wall in back of the altar. My mind was numb. *Nana's really gone!* I thought. Nana had been my confidant. She knew all my fears. She knew my deepest joys. She knew my feelings of how I felt forgotten as the middle child.   Nana knew *me*. There was a bond between us that no one—not even my mother—was aware of. She made me feel special.

I don't know how long I was staring at the crucifix, but I noticed that at the base of the cross, a foggy, white mist was developing. It started out as a swirling, light fog, but as it swirled it became denser. Then someone's feet appeared, and the mist swirled higher, and a glittery white gown became visible. Then it went up even further, and I saw Nana's beaming face. She held her hands out and said, "I'm good! I don't hurt anymore! Don't be sad. Love your mother. She's very upset. I love you. I'll be waiting." Then, with an airmail kiss from her lips, she ascended upward and out of sight. *That's it! I'm going crazy!* I thought. I happened a glance at my mom. She was torn up! She was crying silent tears that rolled down her cheeks, off her chin, and into her Kleenex—poor Mom. I turned my head to look at my aunt. She was sitting there with her mouth hanging open, eyes wide, and tears dripping down her face. My aunt turned to look at me and whispered, "Did you see that?" I wasn't sure what she saw, but I nodded. She grabbed my left hand and squeezed it hard. These memories are assaulting me in rapid succession. *Oh my god*, I thought. *I'm dead!*

I collected myself as much as I could, and Nana said, "Come along. I have *so* much I want to show you!" She took my right hand and we were off. (Literally. Off. Nana would ask me if I wanted to go see or do something, and we were there!) It seemed all one had to do there was think it and *voilà!* You were there!

Our first stop was at a large lake that I could see from where we were standing at the rock. It sat a ways down to the left of the rock, and at the furthest end a huge waterfall was emptying into the lake. I imagined this waterfall was every bit as big as Niagara Falls, if not grander. I had never actually seen Niagara Falls before, but people who had visited there had described it to me as *huge*. The water cascading down into the lake was so clear that from where I stood I could see the stones it was moving over. Beautiful! What set this waterfall apart was not only the immensity of it and the amount of water bubbling into the lake at the base of it but also that there were no deafening echoes of it. I could hear only beautiful melodies coming from it. The strains were not familiar to me, but it was enchanting! Peaceful. Joyous strains! Strong, vibrant, masculine voices blended together in perfect pitch. Being female, I was immediately drawn toward it. *I want that!* I thought. It's pretty hard to describe this feeling, but it was like being witness to absolute, perfect timing and love happening in chorus. Nana and I were sitting on the grass at the edge of this lake and basked in the warmth of all that was around us. Nana closed her eyes and began to sing along with the waterfall. I didn't know she knew a foreign language! It sounded like a combination of all the languages of the world and possibly some heavenly language I had never heard before. They were combined as one to create a melodious, flowing song. It was beautiful! In life, Nana couldn't have carried a tune in a bucket if you had given it to her, but now she had the voice of an angel. I stared at her with my mouth hanging open again. Time was not rushing here. I had no idea how long we were there.

At some point, Nana took my hand and said she needed to show me something next. *Whoosh!* Then we were standing at the edge of a busy cobblestone street. Upon our arrival, I felt like I had been transported to a busy marketplace in Europe. The buildings that lined one side of the street looked like they were made of red bricks. They stood two and three stories high. There were beautiful arched windows with wide windowsills to accommodate every possible kind of potted plant. Some plants were dense and thick with waxy leaves, while others were tall and willowy and housed a large variety of colorful petite flowers. Still others were full and vine-like and draped over the sides of the pots, playing on the constant gentle breezes. Most of the windows had a bevy of colored outdoor awnings. Some were in soft rose colors with gold piping, some were bold and sported a deep maroon with red accent borders, and some were ecru with royal blue piping and borders. The window ledges also provided the array of cats that were among the crowds with a place to sit and groom themselves or just lay on the ledge and watch the goings-on from their perch there.

Everything was manicured, orderly, and so clean. From the open doors of a few buildings, I could see people inside, busily preparing samples of the most delicious delicacies ever assembled in one place. The aroma of these delectable baked goods was as enjoyable as the eating of them. The bakers brought out trays of them to the tables on the street, ready to enjoy. The other side of the street looked out over open meadows where I could see animals of all sorts playing in the grasses there. A small gleaming white fence ran the entire length of the edge of the marketplace. On the other side of this fence, I saw people riding horses, collecting flowers, or lazing in the sun on a blanket. It was such a nice place to be.

People of every age, size, color, and sex were milling around. When I say busy, I mean *busy*. People were elbow to elbow, but it was organized and flowing. No one was being pushed aside. Groups of people were hugging other groups of people. Everyone was smiling, laughing, and enjoying themselves. What *was* this place? I had on my blue corduroy jeans, a white T-shirt, and my favorite pair of sneakers. I had worn these clothes to party in for a day of binge drinking in Vermont. Now, I was embarrassed. My attire was shabby. I had on dark, dirty clothes. The sea of people in this marketplace was dense. There were so many white gowns. Upon my surveying the crowds, I noticed that I wasn't the only one in street clothes. There were a lot of people in dark, dirty clothes as well. Most of them looked as confused as I was. *Where are we?* I wondered. All of us in street clothes were accompanied by at least one person in a white gown. This "marketplace" with all these people, the delicate and constant music, the breezes carrying the aroma of wonderful-smelling baked goods, and all the happy voices of those who gathered here was all comforting and reassuring. However, this was more of a social marketplace where one would not purchase items. Instead, it was a place where one could connect with the other residents and their guests and munch on the variety of sweets and treats that were continually flowing from the ovens to the quaint tables that were everywhere; it was most enjoyable. There was also an abundance of children and animals, all of whom mingled among the crowds.

Dogs of all breeds, shapes, colors, and sizes were receive by everyone they approached who would pet them and show them love. Cats of all varieties, shapes, sizes, and colors were mingling among the crowds too. Some were sitting on windowsills, sunning themselves, or I'd spy some lying in the grasses observing the marketplace and its activities. Some of the people gathered here, young and old alike, would be atop of a horse (without saddles or bridles) and would be threading among the clusters of people, or they would be in the outer area of the marketplace, enjoying a quick run through the surrounding meadows. Such fun! The wildlife was evident everywhere. Squirrels would chase one another up and around the massive trunks of trees.

Fox kits would frolic amid the tall grasses, while deer and cows were peacefully grazing on the lush green land. All the animals seemed to enjoy this activity and approved of it.

Nana brought me here quite often. I would accompany Nana to other places, too. I remember mountain peak leaping with Nana. That was really cool! I remember one of our outings included a seat in an outdoor coliseum. As I took my seat beside Nana, I was awed by the great expanse of this place. There was no roof, and the only enclosed area was where the stage was located. The remaining three areas—where walls would normally be placed—were open and large white opal-looking columns surrounded this meeting place. White doves seemed to constantly glide in and out of this gathering. I noticed that the structure itself was made of huge, ornate stones and looked to be ancient. Large urns of flowers stood lining the area in front of the stage. I remember sitting with Nana and chatting with the others around us. Everyone, including Nana, was eager to hear the message that the speaker, who was seated in a very large throne-like seat in the middle of the stage, was going to deliver on this one occasion. He was very tall and sinewy. On his head was a magnificent, glorious, thick crown of long and flowing pure white hair to the middle of his back. He wore a beautiful white glowing gown with different colored gems lining the hem and cuffs of it. Around his waist, a wide band of dark purple satin was tied in such a way that he looked like a king. His demeanor was one of great wisdom and deserving of respect. He was regal. As he stood to address the crowd, I noticed he carried a large, brown leather book in the crook of his right arm. From this book was the message he delivered. I don't remember his name or the message he had for those in attendance there that day, but I do remember I was captivated by it all.

Nana introduced me to relatives who had passed long before my birth. I have Native American ancestors whom I had the privilege to meet and knew nothing about. There were great aunts and uncles, great grandparents, and first, second, and third cousins who had earthly departed and were now residents of *here*. Then we got into the blood relations of family members twice removed, but they were still kin. And let's not leave out the *by marriage* kinfolk, too. *So* many people. It still makes my head spin!

Nana and I were at the marketplace one time visiting with an elderly couple who were my kin on my great grandmother's side, and I heard my name being called from among the throng of people nearby. I glanced at the crowd of people. No one looked familiar to me. Then suddenly, someone grasped my left arm and gently shook it, much like a child would to get Mama's attention. I turned to see who this could possibly be, and—lo and behold—it was our next-door neighbor from my old neighborhood: *Mr. Z!* He had passed two weeks prior to Memorial Day that year, and he too had lost his battle with cancer. He enfolded me in a big bear hug. It was so good to see him! Oh, he smelled so good. We stepped apart, with him holding my hand in his, and he told me he was doing great. He wanted me to tell his wife, Grammy Z, that he loves her and misses her and that he was waiting for her arrival. He also said to tell her that she should not dwell on his passing, that he was good. I was confused that he should tell me this. Was I the only one who didn't know what was happening and why? Would I be kicked out of here because I didn't belong? Nana had never said I would be leaving, but was this the reason I didn't have a sparkly white gown? Again, my mouth hung open, but I nodded and told him I would. And with that, another quick hug and a peck on my cheek, he disappeared into the flowing throng of people.

Of the many times we visited the marketplace, I had not truly looked at this place and its locale. There was so much to take in with meeting people akin to me. But, this one time, the marketplace seemed rather subdued. It was at this point that I saw the marketplace for what it was. Located in yet another very large, very lush, very bright meadow, the market place was indeed a very large place. It was nestled very quaintly at the base of two extremely tall, luminous mountains. I'd say *mountains* because of their mass and dizzying height. The makeup of these mountains resembled the consistency of dazzling white opal. I could not see through these mountains, but I sensed that another marketplace was just on the other side, out of view. These mountains stood so high that when I tried to see their full height, I almost toppled over backward. From where I stood, the furthest reaches of these mountains were wafted by the same misty clouds I'd descended through upon my arrival there. How tall were these things anyway? Another surprise that was evident—but not initially noticed on my part—was that there were two very wide strips of gleaming gold that stretched the entire length of this one particular mountain. Gates? The ever-present golden light would glint off the gold strips and lend a beautiful glow to the whole area. Simply beautiful! Why were there gates on a mountainside?

The air held an aroma of sweet, spicy, tangy pine, and freshly-washed linens all combined to lend an even more comforting and pleasurable atmosphere to my experience of the marketplace. All scents were identifiable alone and combined together for an amazingly comforting, tranquil, spa-like sensation. I really enjoyed coming to the marketplace. Although I don't recall how many times I was there at the marketplace, I know that we—Nana and I—went there often, and it was an ever-pleasant place to go to and enjoy. There were times when I would stroll off to the outer circle of this amazing place and find myself a quiet place to sit, observe, and contemplate the goings-on around me and wonder, *Why was I here?*

Nana and I were back at the rock, (the one she was atop of when I first arrived). We were sitting on a level plane in the rock holding hands and silently enjoyed our time together. Compatible silence. Neither one of us seemed inclined to talk. Nana released my hand suddenly and stood up. She came to stand in front of me. Her eyes told me she had something important to tell me. I straightened myself up and looked back into her eyes. She seemed to be at a loss for words. I waited in silence. She cleared her throat with a little cough and said, "I need to leave you here. I have some appointments that you cannot accompany me to. I'll be back shortly." And with that, *Poof!* She was gone. I didn't even get a chance to ask her "Why not?" Then total and absolute blackness descended around me. I could see nothing.

Until this moment, darkness had never descended on this place. I was terrified! I'd venture to say that this blackness was so complete that I could *feel* it. It was all- consuming, almost to the extent of sucking the oxygen out of the atmosphere. My only thought was, *Don't move off this rock!* I didn't. In fact, I plastered myself across the rock so that every possible part of my body was touching it. What was happening? I couldn't see a thing. I held my hand before my face, and it was not visible. My breathing was becoming shallow and hard to draw. *Nana!* I'm so scared! *Why was this happening? Where did Nana go? Why am I here alone?* Zillions of unanswered questions rifled through my mind. I had heard some people talk before about the abyss, this large black eternal hole in the universe. *Was this what this was? Will I never see light again? Am I doomed to suffer, terrified in this blackness for eternity? Was this hell?* I screamed for Nana. And again. All the lovely sounds of the meadow were gone, replaced by angry hissing sounds. The tranquil scents were replaced by acrid, offensive odors. Suddenly, I heard Nana's voice calling my name from the other side of the rock. I listened hard for Nana's voice again. It came calling my name. "Darlene, come to the other side of the rock. Take my hand. I'll take you from this darkness. Trust me! Take my hand. Let go of the rock! *Trust me!*" Nana's beckoning to me went on and on. No way was I letting go of this rock! It was the only reality in this black world that I could hold on to. I began crawling around the rock like a crab would crawl around in the sand, never stepping off of the rock. I needed to see Nana. Why did she leave me here alone in the first place, only to beckon me to her on the other side of the rock from which we sat beforehand? This did not make sense.

While I was crawling crab-like around to the other side of the rock, I sensed that I was getting there. I dared to look to my right. The only thing I could see in this blackness was a very tiny pinpoint of light far off. I trained my eyes to it. Light! Nana's voice seemed to be coming from this pinpoint of light. What? A full body shudder shook my body. This was not right. I looked away from the light. Nana's voice assaulted me now with an intensity to it of becoming hysterical, "Darlene! Let go of the rock! Come to the light? Take my hand! Now! Take my hand, now!" No way, José! The pinpoint of light began to grow in size. It was getting closer to me. I looked at it again and saw a silhouette of a person in it. Nana? It resembled Nana, but was it? I remained stuck to the rock like a starfish. The light was hovering in front of me just an arm's length away. My eyes started to ache, because it was a glaring, intrusive sort of light. There was nothing reassuring or comforting about having this light only a feet in front of me. I was unable to see Nana clearly, although the figure within this circle of light was still calling me. Nana's voice was still urging me to let go of the rock. "Trust me," the voice said. "Take my hand."

At some point in this verbal assault, I had lowered my head into the crook of my left arm, which was on the rock. I needed to think about this. Why didn't I trust Nana's pleas enough to let go of this rock? Why did this feeling of total uncertainty keep bubbling in my gut to not trust this person? Wasn't she a resident here now? So, what was the problem? It seemed to me that the foul odors that had started to permeate this tranquil place at the beginning of this black period were then so strong it became hard to breathe. I realized that I was trying not to breathe in this foul stench. "Oh, man, this reeks!" I said. I was going to throw up. The air quality was that of days-old fish and sewage. I mean this was a stink-bomb! This stench far exceeded the smell I had experienced in my kitchen when I saw that hideous creature just a few days before.

Still, the verbal onslaught continued. I saw Nana's outstretched hand from within the light. Her voice had taken on an unnatural sound. This couldn't be! Now, all I wanted to do was get away and seek the safety and shelter from the other side of the rock. I was having difficulty holding onto the rock. My senses were reeling, and I wasn't so sure I could make it back to the other side. "Let go of the rock! Take my hand!" was the only thing I could hear. The stench was circling around me as if to detach me from the rock. I felt finger-like things on my body—pushing, pulling, preying fingers. I summoned every ounce of what energy was left in me and screamed, *"Nooooo! You are not my Nana! Leave me alone! I will not take your hand!"* Instantaneously, the darkness lightened to a hazy blur of my surroundings. There was nothing beautiful about this place. Everything in the surrounding meadow where Nana and I had just been sitting on the rock was dead, withered, and stinking. The light within the sphere lessened its intensity, and the silhouette was now visible. The figure who was standing before me looked very much like the being who had appeared in my kitchen that one day and was definitely not my Nana. Rather, it was hideous-looking.

This was not female; it was definitely male. However, this was not at all like any males I had ever seen. He was extremely tall and practically filled the space of light. His breathing was jagged and labored. He was glaring at me with tangible hatred emanating from his veiled eyes. On his huge head it seemed his hair was seething. It had a life of its own! Hundreds if not thousands of creepy, crawling vipers lurched out at me. They recoiled back to his head only to lurch out at me again and again. They had long, stained, filthy fangs in their mouths. His dried-out, scab-encrusted lips stretched over his slim, covered teeth. Now, as I remember this, his mouth and teeth reminded me of the Dr. Seuss cartoon, "How the Grinch Stole Christmas," only he was so much more evil looking.

It was all I could do not to faint from sheer terror. His garb was moth-eaten, foul-smelling, bedraggled ribbons of dried out, leather-like strips wrapped around his torso and shoulders. His legs looked like dried out bones of human beings that had been broken and were secured with rotting flesh. The odor was now so pungent that it hurt my whole being. His feet were shod with what looked like rotting human beings. I saw human faces there that were all howling. They were twisted and wrapped around his ankles. Their loose hands were flailing around, groping for something other than his legs. His hand was still outstretched before me. Extending from his grotesque hands were the longest and ugliest fingernails I had ever seen. They were very, very long, filthy dirty, stained blood red, sharp, and jagged. I couldn't take my eyes off this hideous creature.

He gestured for me to come with his index finger and was shouting at me in an ominous, dangerous voice. "Let go of the rock!" I couldn't breathe! Once again, it took all my strength to scream, *"Noooo!"* A mighty wind began assaulting me, as if to fling me off the rock.

His head jerked back and I could see his eyes. They were like shark eyes, the color of putrid green. His head was now tilted completely back, and he let out one of the most utterly terrifying screams I had ever heard. It seemed he would never stop screaming. He was screaming so loud that the rock I was clinging to shifted under me. The ground all around me was heaving, and, if possible, the air was filled with an even more horrific smell. I clutched the rock like someone holding onto a life preserver in a pitching ocean. I buried my head into the crook of my left arm on the rock. I was finally able to look away. His screeching finally ended, and his head came back into an upright position. His hate-filled green eyes were trained on me. His face was distorted into another ghoulish appearance. His body was bulked up, and he was even larger than I first thought. Massive. Giant-like. He opened his scab-encrusted mouth and directed his breath at me. More rancid, death-smelling odors engulfed me. I was coughing, crying, and clutching the rock so hard I thought my arms were going to break. *I'll let go of the rock!* I thought. *Noooo!* Cold sweat had soaked my clothes and was running down my face. I was so weak. Terror was coursing through my body. *He's going to kill me!* was all I could think. The time to fight the good fight was *now*. If I had allowed myself to let go of the rock, I don't know what would have happened to me! I summoned every last bit of strength, energy, and faith that I had and screamed again, *"Nooo!"* The stench was engulfing me. Squeezing my chest to the point of collapsing, I let out another strangled scream. *"Nooo!"*

Abruptly, everything stopped. Everything. No more howling voices were coming from his feet. No more hissing sounds. The air around him was vibrating, sending off more smell. It was dangerously quiet. He leaned toward me, towering over me. In a malicious, quiet tone, he said, "So, you think I'm going to let you go *now?* You are *never* going to escape me! I've had you by your short hairs for quite some time. It's inevitable. You're *mine!*" He continued his tyrannical speech and proceeded to tell me all the things, words, and actions I had done; I knew they were wrong, but I had still chosen to do them. The lies I had told my parents and others, the alcohol and drug use over my recent past, the mean actions toward my brothers, every large and small wrong I had ever done. He continued, "You, my dear, belong to *me!*" I was now plastered, as best I could be, to the rock. I was gasping and gulping for air, fighting the terror that had consumed me and that I had desperately been trying to make sense of. *Oh, dear God! Help me!* I raised my head from my arm, still gasping for air, and I looked at him with my own hardened eyes and manage to rasp out, "*You* are a liar! I do not belong to you! You are not my Nana and I *will not* let go of this rock, and I *will not* follow you!" A hair-raising, flesh-pimpling, ear-splitting scream erupted from him like a volcano that had lain dormant for years. His whole body was shuddering, and the ground began to tremble again. He was still in the throes of his horrific scream, and the light started a rapid retreat. Before he disappeared from my sight, he screamed at me, "You're mine! You cannot escape *me!*" There was total darkness once again for a nanosecond. I collapsed against the rock, sobs wracking my body. *Where's Nana?* I thought. As if on cue, Nana was back, cradling me in her arms. She was purring words of love and comfort, wiping my face with the sleeve of her white gown. She continued to stroke my head and face and kissed my cheeks. Hey! The lights came back on. Cool!

We were once again in the lush, green meadow, sitting on the side of the rock. There was no trace of the foul stench. Everything was like new. We sat. Nana was rocking me back and forth like she did when I was a child. Nana! Oh, she smelled *so* good. She was hushing my sobs. Words of endearment were flowing over me, comforting my fear. I don't know how long we sat there. The atmosphere felt like it had a different character. I felt it and sensed it. I didn't know why there had been this change in the atmosphere. *Will I be cast out of here anyway?* I wondered. I knew I wasn't staying there with Nana. It couldn't be so! I turned to face Nana and reached for her face with my hands. It was like I wanted to etch the feel of her into my memory. I looked deep into her eyes questioningly, but didn't voice my question: "Am I leaving you?" Nana was smiling, but her sparkling eyes were not as sparkly as before, and they held a forlorn sadness in their depths. She simply said, "It's time for you to go."

"Wait! What? Right now?" I answered. "No, Nana! I want to stay here with *you!*" Tears began flowing out of my eyes and down my cheeks. My hands dropped to her forearms, where she was holding me by my waist. I grasped her arms and gave them a little shake. Nana touched my right cheek in a loving caress. She said, "You have to go back! It's not your time! You have much work to do."

I pleaded with her, "No. I want to stay here with *you!* Can't I please stay?"

Nana said, "Oh, darlin', I'd love for you to stay! But what about your parents? They'll surely miss you! Won't you miss them? And what about your boyfriend, Tom? What's he supposed to do without you? You're ready to leave him alone, without you to love him? And your true friends? What about them?" I pondered her questions for a minute and then answered, "They'll all adjust. I want to stay with you!" What was the big deal? It's not like I'd been a model human being. I had many flaws. Maybe they would be better off without me around. Nana was looking at me with sad eyes now and said, "You can't. There's much work you have to do. You're not finished yet."

"What work?" I asked. "Finish what?"

Nana continued her explanation. "If you stay, *you will not stay!*" As she said that, she gripped my lower arms that were still clutching her lower arms, and she shook them as she said those last four words. She shook them gently but firmly.

"You mean always?" I asked.

"No. I mean *now*," she answered.

A glimmer of hope was rising in my chest. "So if I agree to go back now, when I come back here I can stay?" I asked.

"Yes, sweetheart!" Nana answered emphatically

Well, that was some consolation. I didn't want Nana to leave me behind, but rather it was me who would be departing. I swallowed the tears forming in my throat and said, "Okay." Before I could finish what else I wanted to say to Nana, there was a tremendously loud clap of thunder.

Chapter 4

BACK TO MY PHYSICAL REALITY!

Darlene

I awoke suddenly with a start. My eyes flew open. I was startled to *not* see our bedroom. Instead of waking and seeing the Led Zeppelin "Stairway to Heaven" poster that hung on our bedroom wall directly in front of my side of the bed, I saw a glaring white ceiling and a large curtainless window through which I could see a large desk and office chairs. A woman garbed in a crisp white nurse's uniform and cap was at the foot of the strange bed I was lying in, and she was checking various glass bottles that hung from metal poles. From these bottles were clear plastic lines that ran from them to the foot of the bed.

My first thought was, *Where the hell am I now?* So I voiced that thought out loud. The nurse jumped and spun around. Her eyes were practically popping out of her head, and her mouth looked as if it were unhinged. She excitedly asked me, "What did you say?"

"Where the hell am I?" I repeated.

I felt as if I were talking around a mouthful of marbles, and whose *voice* was that? Was there a man in here who I didn't see? And if so, how did he know what I wanted to say? And why the hell was it so hard to talk? The nurse abandoned the bottles and ran up by the side of the bed. She stood looking at me as if she couldn't believe I could speak. She replied, "You're in the General Hospital, the Intensive Care Unit." I knew I had heard of that place before, but where was that? She continued. "You were in a serious car accident on Memorial Day." I was having a hard time being back in the physical. I then had a flashback of sorts and remembered that Tom and Bob, a friend of ours, and I had gone to Vermont with our next door neighbor, "Beep," to spend the day bar hopping. Beep belonged to several fraternities there, and we could drink for much less than at a regular bar! So we went.

I looked at her and said, "Ahhh, we didn't make it home from our day out?"

"No," she answered. "All three of you are lucky to be alive!"

"Tom? Bob?" I asked.

"They're okay," she said. "You're the one who was DOA on the scene. Paramedics and an ER nurse, who had just gotten off work from the local hospital in Vermont, stabilized you until you could be transported first to the local hospital then here to the General Hospital in New Hampshire. You're a miracle to be alive!"

"Wow," I said.

This sounded serious. Why didn't I remember any of it? I know I drank a *lot* at our party, and I sort of remembered where that was, but, where was *here*?

There was silence for a minute except for the beeping and whooshing sounds coming from all the machines that surrounded my bed. My mind was racing in all sorts of directions at once. *Where was Tom now? Was he really okay? Bob! Was he okay, really? Where are they now? Could I see them? My parents! Did they know what was happening? Had someone called them yet? What day was this? And, what the hell was in my throat and mouth? It was seriously annoying!*

While my mind was dismantling, reorganizing, and trying desperately to wrap around the fact that I was *here* and Nana wasn't, the nurse asked me, "What is your name?" It took a couple of heartbeats to fully understand the simple question of what my name was. I asked her, "How long have I been here?"

"Just about two weeks," was the reply. "*And* you don't know *my name!*" (It's hard to be indignant when you have what feels like a mouth full of shit and you'd like to blister them with some snappy verbiage!) Wait a minute, two weeks here ... how could a nurse, who is, this minute, fiddling with IV bottles and is evidently in charge of caring for me *not know my bloody name?* Her response was: "Well, I don't always work in the Intensive Care Unit. The first time I saw you was when you were brought in by ambulance on Memorial Day evening. I really thought that I would never take care of you again. You were a total mess! So, no I don't know your name, and I cannot see your chart at the foot of the bed from here to read your name ..."

"Darlene LaCroix," I told her.

The fact that I was Darlene LaCroix—and that I *knew* I was Darlene LaCroix—was a very big deal to this woman. She did a little happy dance and clapped her hands once.

"Okay. Where am I again?" I asked.

"General Hospital in New Hampshire, near the college and hockey rink."

"Oookaaay ... where's that?" I asked.

"Near the hockey rink."

"Yeah, where's that?" I asked. "Next to the college?"

"Near Rich's department store," she answered.

The light bulb came on now. Rich's, I thought. "Okay, I know where that is!"

The nurse was so excited she was jumping up and down. She told me in a rushed voice, "I'll be right back!" and she ran from the room like her hair was on fire.

I was left alone in a strange room in a strange bed, and I was thinking how very odd it was that she had left in such a hurry. Oh well. Medical people tend to be that way, right? My eyes traveled from the now empty doorway to the foot of the bed I was in. Two IV poles with two glass IV bottles on each were stationed in front of each side of the bed. From the bottles, the IV lines led to the foot of the bed and into each of my lower legs and feet. The sheet covering the bed was folded back to expose the lower half of both my legs. I counted two needles plugged into each of my legs *and* both feet. My eyes left the foot of my bed, and I realized that my pj's (a hospital johnny) were not *on* me, but rather were draped over the upper portion of my body (shoulders to hips). A white sheet covered me from my knees to my chest, and a blue blanket was over that.

The next thing I saw was that both of my arms were encased in black sleeve-like looking thingies. I counted four needles in my right arm and three in my left. I wanted to move my arms and feet, but they would not move. (Oh my God! What did my hair look like?) While I was distracted about the condition of my hair, the nurse who had just raced from my room came back in and with her were a *lot* of people, both men and women. Upon entering, a sea of white lab coats filed into the room and around my bed. In their arms, they all carried a notebook and were sporting large, curious eyes, all of which were trained on me! What the—? Was I a lab experiment or something? Who the hell were all these people? The oldest looking lab coat person spoke up and introduced himself. "Hello, Darlene. I'm Dr. Jones, and

I am the doctor in charge of you while you stay at General Hospital. These young people with me are medical students, and, if you don't mind, we'd like to ask you a few questions. When you've had enough, just let me know and we'll leave, okay?"

Well, what could I have said? I had a mouthful of shit, and where the hell was I going to go? He seemed nice enough, though. He had kind eyes. "Okay, somebody *please* get this shit out of my throat and mouth! I can't talk, and it's starting to piss me off!" I said.

There were questions. Hundreds of them, from everyone! (1) What's your name? (*Weren't you listening?*) (2) Where do you live? (3) What are your parents' names? (4) Do you know why you're here? (5) Do you have any brothers or sisters? Answers: (1) Darlene LaCroix. (2) I live over a market in New Hampshire. (3) My parents are Leon and Thelma LaCroix. (4) I was in a car accident? (5) I have three brothers, one older and two younger. On and on, mostly the same questions. I felt like I was being interrogated. The only thing missing was a rubber hose and a big guard named Bubba! How many more hours of this? (In actuality it was about fifteen to twenty minutes of questioning.) But it felt like hours.

I was getting tired. And I had a mouthful of whatever it was that was impeding my ability to talk. It was extremely tiring. My eyes were getting heavy, and I wanted to go back to sleep. I wanted to be with Nana. As if from a distance, I heard Dr. Jones tell me he would be back a little later. I heard swooshing and ruffling—like autumn leaves that had lingered on the branches until they were dried out and brown—as the doc and a sea of lab coats left my bedside. No more questions! There was silence except for the continual beeping of the machines around me. I was able to raise my eyelids a notch and could see the cluster of lab coats out in the hall. They surrounded Dr. Jones. He was talking to them, and they were all scribbling furiously in their notebooks and glancing back at me. I let my eyes close. Ahhh! Sweet sleep. Nana? Where were you?

I was in and out of sleep. I felt like I was in a constant fog. I didn't know if I was awake or dreaming. My parents, brothers, and a Catholic priest floated through my mind. The priest was performing the last rites on me. I remember thinking, *No! I was sent back here! You're wasting perfectly good Holy Water and salt. I'm back. Much to my chagrin, I'm back.*

Images of nurses, doctors, medical students, housekeeping, my parents, and Tom floated through my mind. Were they real? I felt funky. And what the hell was in my throat and mouth? Was I doomed to live with this intrusion forever? I couldn't talk. Sleepiness was a constant. I would have liked to be able to sit up a bit. I was sick and tired of looking at the ceiling and counting the holes. (Now I knew how many holes it took to fill the ICU hall.)

Sleep was my ever-present companion. Sometimes, sleeping was not how I wanted to spend all my time. I had questions I not only wanted but *needed* to have answered! Questions like: Why couldn't I move? Would I ever get out of this bed? Would someone, anyone, *please* take this shit out of my mouth and throat? Why was it there? As I lay there in a strange bed in the ICU, I had begun remembering the day of the crash. Bits and pieces of the events that had taken place that fateful day were rampaging through my mind. I knew where I was at the start of the day—in my kitchen with Tom and our friend, Bob. I remembered our landlord bringing up a quarter keg that was still almost full that had been returned to his store earlier that morning, and he had also brought bags of ice to set the keg up in our kitchen sink. I recalled that all four of us began drinking before seven am. I vaguely remember my younger brother coming to our apartment to ask us to come to a cookout at my parents' later that day. When he came to our apartment, we were already on our way to being drunk. I remembered Beep coming to our apartment and asking us if we wanted to go to Vermont and drink the day away at the fraternity he belonged to there. I remembered being so drunk that I couldn't stand to dance, and when I tried, I fell to the floor several times in a drunken heap. I remembered asking Bob if he could drive when we left that last bar. As we began our journey home, Bob began hysterically laughing and matting the gas pedal to the floorboard in his little yellow Fiat. Each time he did, he would rear back his head and emit a terrifying howl of laughter. I was scared to death! I remembered flying along the narrow road parallel to the Connecticut River and screaming at Bob to slow down. All the while, Bob still laughed hysterically. I recall that Tom yelled at me to stop yelling at Bob. We then turned on to an even narrower road in the middle of the little town that was closest to where we lived in New Hampshire. Bob was driving like a madman, and I heard the tires screeching as we somehow made it around the small bends in that road. I felt sheer panic when I saw the hairpin turn lying in wait on the road before us. I grabbed Tom's upper left arm and screamed for Bob to slow down. Tom was in the front passenger bucket seat while I sat in the back seat. I saw the distance between three obstacles certain to cause death rapidly coming at us. On the right was a small mobile home, and slightly in front of that was a cluster of dense trees. To the left of that were the wooden guard rails that stood at the edge of the hairpin turn. I remembered looking up and saying, "Dear God, if you any mercy at all, let us get through this alive." I then put my head down into the crook of my left arm on the back of the seat Tom was sitting in. I had no memories of the actual crash, as I had lost consciousness at that time. My next sequences of memories were of not being in my physical body, but that of spending time with my deceased Nana, of a beautiful picturesque place where she resides, and having to leave that place and come back into my physical body.

I had much time to think about what I experienced after waking up in the ICU. The few times I dared to tell anyone, a couple of nurses, about my experience being on the other side and walking with my deceased Nana, they told me it was a hallucination. They would tell me it was all a hallucination caused by the heavy pain and sleep medications I was on and also because I had been in a coma for two weeks. That explanation did not satisfy me then. I knew I had been drinking when the car crash happened, but the immediate sensation of being an observer of the scene was indeed long before I was fished out of the stream twenty-two minutes after the accident. I was blue from head to foot and showed no vital signs at all. I was not on any heavy pain or sleeping medication then. I did not feel any pain while I was there with my Nana, and I was very much aware of the events prior to the crash.

My religious instruction before now had been to believe in something larger than myself, in something that was not tangible on earth. I had learned I would have to wait until I physically died to experience it, and that heaven was going to be all I experienced. So, why were all the people who believed in life after death—and who have been continuously teaching and telling me of heaven all my life—*now* saying to me it that it was a result of medication? I did not believe them. It was very, very, real. I longed to be back with Nana again.

One morning I was lying in bed staring at the ceiling, and all I could think about was how uncomfortable the bed was and how comfortable the Geri-chair against the wall looked. The door to the room opened, and a younger looking male in a white lab coat approached my bed. He was a resident doctor from the pulmonary functions department. He introduced himself, but his name escapes me now. He then asked me if I would like to have this—and he wiggled the tube that was up my nose and down into my throat—removed today. Well, hell yeah! He then said that I would probably feel a slight pinch in the back of my throat, but that it shouldn't be too bad. On the count of three … ready? One, two, three, *snap, pull.* There was pressure in my nose and throat, and a sudden burning and severe pain radiated from the back of my throat and neck. Ribbed plastic tubing was being pulled (and none too gently) out of my right nostril. When the tube was 99 percent out of my nose, an explosion of blood spurted from my mouth, followed by a steady stream of blood from my nose. "Pain?" you ask. Well, *yeah!*

I vaguely remembered that two nurses came into the room at the same time the doc from pulmonary functions did. They each went to either side of my bed and busied themselves with checking IV bottles, IV sites, IV lines, and other various medical equipment. The nurse on the right side of my bed must have untethered my right arm from the black sleeve-like thingy, because when the tube removal was at its most painful apex and blood was spurting everywhere, my right hand—by itself—had grabbed hold of the doc's throat in a death grip. Through the blood, which was now a steady current, I sputtered, "You lying son of a bitch! That hurt like hell!" Instantly, both nurses grabbed my right hand, which was trying to squeeze the life out of the doc via his throat, and they wrestled with me to unclench my grip. The funny thing is that I saw neither hide nor hair of that particular doc for the remainder of my stay there. Excruciating, searing-hot pulsating pain radiated from the front of my throat to the back of my nose. Blood covered the front of me and the bed. It was then that I realized I was sitting up in bed. Cool!

The amount of blood that was on me, the bed, the floor, and the nurses shocked me. Was I going to hemorrhage and die painfully this time? Would I see Nana again? What about Tom? I needed to tell him I loved him and didn't blame him for the car accident! I sensed that Tom would have blamed himself for our going so far away from home for a day of binge drinking. It was just how he thought. He had told me many times that he would put his own life in danger to save me from any type of harm.

While hundreds of similar thoughts clogged my mind—all at the same time—I began to gag, and more blood was making its way out of my mouth and nose. How much blood does it take to suffocate, anyway? And how many pints of blood were there in the human body? It looked like there were at least two gallons of it on me and on my bed! I was simply amazed at how quickly the nurses had changed my IV bottles, my johnny, and placed a large gauze pad under my chin to absorb rogue dribbles of blood from my mouth and nose. And they changed the bed, too! They coaxed me to lay back on the bed. The taste of blood was still on my tongue. My upper chest and throat were still burning. Would it ever stop? What was happening now? A trickle of blood escaped from my lips and ran down over my chin onto the fresh gauze pad. The neck of my recently-changed johnny was soaked with a new trickle of blood from my mouth. *Whoosh!* The nurses changed my blood-soaked johnny and gauze pad with lightning speed. They moved in unison like a well-oiled machine! They finished entering data into my chart at the foot of the bed and spoke in medical lingo, which sounded Greek to me. I was checked and double-checked, and then I saw it—the syringe. Every time a nurse had that in her hand, I would go to sleep. Yup, *boom, boom,* the lights began to fade, the pulsating pain in my neck and throat started to dissipate ... *zzz.*

When I was first admitted to General Hospial on Sunday, May 28, it was decided that I would be kept as still as possible. I had to have emergency abdominal surgery because I was losing blood pressure and there was no apparent reason (such as deep and bleeding lacerations, etc.) for it, so Dr. Jones ordered exploratory surgery of my abdomen to "take a look." Apparently, a significant amount of broken glass was in my abdomen, causing internal bleeding. That, of course, was the perpetrator for the blood pressure loss. A few snips and tucks and I would be good as used.

Upon examination of the X-rays of my chest, abdomen, arms, and legs, it was clear that several of my ribs were cracked—and some were broken—and my lungs were at least 70 percent full of water. A New Hampshire state patrolman had found me in the stream with my face stuck down at the bottom of it, and I had breathed in the muck and mire there, which now clogged my lungs. *Great.* The X-rays also showed that one of the cracked ribs was so cracked that if I moved around too much, it would break at an angle, puncturing my right lung and causing severe (if not life-threatening) bleeding, enough to cause suffocation and death.

My Mom came to visit me one time, and I was in a hazy state of consciousness. I was not very comfortable. Mom said I was trying to ask for help with something about my bed, but I was not able to speak very well. My throat, tongue, and lips were not cooperating so as to speak. If my memory serves me correctly, they felt like they had been welded shut. So I was "signing" my responses to her questions with my hands. I had learned American Sign Language from a young deaf man I had dated a few years earlier before I met Tom. Neither my mom nor any of the ICU nurses knew sign language. A very long guessing game of what I was signing about ensued. It was totally frustrating for all parties! Note to medical people: *learn basic sign language.*

My chest heaved, my breathing was labored, my throat felt like there was a vice locked around it and was being squeezed shut, and my eyes fluttered closed. From "out there" I could hear women's voices, shrill and frantic, and I heard paper ripping, Suddenly, my whole body convulsed, and it felt like my chest just caved in. The screeching sound grew faint, and I was engulfed in utterly still darkness.

I had had an unexpected second heart attack. The first heart attack was expected, and all heart-related machines/equipment, re-fib, oxygen, paddles, etc., were at the ready, and the first incident was quickly averted. This second heart attack, however, was absolutely not expected and took everyone by complete surprise. I really don't remember much about it—only that I was terrified. As I spent days staring at the ceiling and thinking about my experience on the other side, I so wanted with every fiber of my being to be there instead of here. I could smell Nana around me, but I couldn't see her. I missed the comfort, the smells, the beauty of the place and all things there. I missed everything about being there. I felt like that was my home. I *know* that place was my home. Time was just that: *time.* There was no rushing anywhere or feeling like one had to be somewhere for anything except for the joy of just being. Being in the hospital, in this physical place, was uncomfortable. Everything in the physical realm was so hard. I wanted to experience the joy of being able to think about doing something or going somewhere, and *poof!* I would be in midst of it. I didn't have to struggle to experience the things I desired to do. Everything was immediate. There were no time constraints. Worrying was non-existent. I missed the contentment of feeling complete and of feeling worthy to exist. While there, I never felt like I was being judged.

Dr. Jones entered with a huge grin on his face. He stopped at the foot of my bed to look at my chart. He still had that grin on his face. He closed the chart, greeted me and my parents, and then shook my Dad's hand. He then told the three of us that I was being moved to the seventh floor. I was leaving the ICU. I was doing "wonderfully." I would be there a few more days. Then *home! Yippee-yi-o-kyi-yayyyy!*

I would be sedated awhile longer. Everything was healing, but I still needed to be semi-quiet. I would have a room with a view! The move was on. The nurse's aide came in, and off we went, seventh floor bound.

Chapter 5

MY NEW VIEW

Darlene

The view from the gurney I was on when we entered my new room was *wunderbar!* Three huge windows filled the opposite wall. There was lots of light, and my bed was right in front of them, *Yessa!* When I reached my new bed and settled in, I looked out the window and realized that I had truly missed the simple pleasure of looking out the window while being in the ICU. I knew it was a small pleasure, but it was huge to me—memorable!

It was still a few days until the official date that summer began, in June, 1978. That meant I was there for almost four weeks. The sun was shining, and a few late-blooming lilac trees that lined one of the entrances to the hospital filled the drifting breezes with the last of their fragrances. I had a date with two nurses to walk to the bathroom, wash up and brush my teeth, and then go back to bed. I was so excited. This would be the first time I would get out of bed and could see what my hair actually looked like. I weighed a whopping seventy-eight pounds. I stood, wobbly knees and all, but I was vertical. Yippee! I clutched the nurse's hand to my left and had a hold of the IV pole in my right. The second nurse was behind me with a wheelchair.

The three of us began the trek across my room toward the bathroom. Who moved the bathroom fifty miles from my bed? It was amazing how quickly the human body weakens from only lying in a bed. My knees involuntarily knocked as I placed one foot in front of the other to get to the bathroom. I was exhausted, and we weren't even to the end of the bed yet. Yikes! This endeavor could have either taken a very long time or I was going to die in the process. We finally arrived at the bathroom doorway, and I really needed to sit down. I felt like I had just participated in a 10K race. There was a mirror over the sink. The person who was looking back at me from the mirror was a complete stranger. Who the hell was *that?* I saw the shoulder-length blondish hair of a young woman, extremely large brown eyes, hollow cheeks, and a chicken neck looking back at me. I blinked, and "she" blinked. I blinked again, and so did she. *Oh my God!* That was *me!*

I was slender before, but this person looked like a starvation survivor. My arms were the size of toothpicks, I could clearly see my shoulder bones, and I had no ass. I needed to sit down. The shock of seeing myself as the first living skeleton with skin was traumatizing. Thank God my face wasn't busted up—I only had a few scratches and some bruising on my chin and forehead—or I'd have really freaked. This was *not* the body I was used to. The funny thing is that I hadn't noticed my condition before this. We finished up in the bathroom, and it took all my strength to do this. I was tired. I needed to get back into bed. I needed to ask Nana, "Was this really necessary? Was this part of "the plan"?

My mind began racing again in all sorts of directions at once. *Why?* I thought. *What was the point of experiencing this?* I asked myself the biggest question of all: *If I told people, especially medical* people, about my being on the "other side," would I be put into a padded room for the rest of my life? Who was going to believe me? The sanctuary of my bed loomed ahead. I really felt the need to talk to my Nana!

Later that morning, I awoke from my nap, and the nurse who was changing my IV bottle smiled and told me that a girl named Becki called and wanted to know if I could have visitors. She would be arriving shortly. Yea! A friendly face that I know! My best friend in the whole wide world would be coming to see me. I made another grueling trip to the bathroom so I wouldn't look like hell. Becki could *not* see my hair like this! As I brushed my teeth this time, I realized that I had all my teeth. None were lost in the car wreck. *Yeehaw!* I ran a comb through my hair and trekked back to bed. I asked for a clean johnny and was ready for my first visit with my BFF. As I lay in my bed waiting for Becki to come, I had some time to think about my visit to the other side and wondered if she would she think I was completely nuts if I told her I had been in heaven.

Becki arrived a short time later. She was a sight for sore eyes— mine! She was carrying a gift bag, a plant of some sort, and she had chocolate. (I firmly believe chocolate should be its own food group!) Over her shoulder she had a leather saddlebag purse with a long leather fringe, which I had been secretly hoping she would get tired of and give to me. And, of course, she looked great. I watched her walk into the room, her face mirroring, for just a second, the thought I had had when I first saw myself in the mirror earlier. *Wow! You look like shit!* There was a slight hitch in her giddy-up after she spotted me, but she recovered her stride and proceeded to fling everything but the plant onto my bed. We embraced. Oh, she smelled so good. Sunshine and vanilla! She was already tanned and the picture of health. She was sporting yet another new summer outfit; the girl was a clotheshorse.

Her hair was longer than I remembered, and she looked awesome. Ugh, she was always the cutest one of our duo.

I wasn't sure where to begin. So we chatted about the weather, mutual friends, and of course, the car accident. The truth about the car accident was that I didn't remember the crash because when I saw that we were going to hit any one of the three things I saw from the window, I thought we were all going to die. Becki was staring at me. I know I looked a fright. My voice was like that of a stranger. My appearance was scary, and I think she was scared of me. I'm the one who knew how she peed her pants laughing too hard and how she was unable to control it. "Please, don't look at me like that," I told her. "You're scaring me! What did *they* tell you before you came in?" I managed to swallow the panic.

Becki was jumpy. She couldn't seem to find a comfortable way to sit. She busied herself unwrapping the plant and placed it on the windowsill. Did I want some chocolate? *Yes!* We were eating chocolate, and I wondered if I should broach the "other-side experience" then or wait. I decided to wait. I would have liked, at least, one more visit with her before she decided I'm a total nut job and faded from my life. The thought of losing my BFF caused more panic. If she decided this was enough and she couldn't handle me as her friend anymore, who could I bare my soul to? Who knew the things about me that only she knew? (We took a blood oath about that.)

I proceeded to tell Becki that I wasn't sure if Tom wanted me anymore. I hadn't seen him or heard from him in days, and the rejection by both Becki and Tom would have been devastating. Did I really want to live without Becki? My whole being was invested in this friendship. She was my "soul sista"! *No!* Becki would *never* understand my being on the other side and walking with my Nana! It was settled; I was sure I was a freak.

We visited awhile longer. She caught me up to speed with what was going on at home before getting ready to leave. I really didn't want her to leave. I didn't want to be alone. She didn't want to leave either, but her Mom needed her car. She promised she would be back real soon. I needed my rest, and—after her kiss, kiss, hug, hug—she left. Shit! I was tired, but could not get comfy. My chest ached, my throat felt sore, and I had a headache. I saw Nana's smiling face just inches from mine before I drifted off to sleep. She was stroking my head and whispered to me, "That's right. Just sleep now. You'll be fine. I love you!"

Someone was gently nudging my shoulder. I heard my name being called. "Darlene. Daaaarlene. *Darleeeenee!*" I opened one eye enough to see who, if anyone, was there, and it was my Dad. Leon LaCroix. He sat in a chair by my bed, *and* he had more *chocolate.* Good Dad! He was on his lunch break from working at the hospital in Vermont, just a stone's throw away from mine in New Hampshire. It was good to see him. I was the reason for his rapidly graying hair and the loss of that hair, as he'd told me on several occasions. Dad eyeballed me and said, "You look good."

"What?" I answered. "I look good? Dad, you need to get a new pair of glasses! Really, I look like a starved chicken with no ass! But if you think I look *good*, well then—you're entitled to your opinion."

Dr. Manning came in, took my vitals, and nodded his head as if satisfied. Before he left, Dad asked if he could have a word with him in the hall. *What's this?* I wondered. *Something everyone was not telling me? I'm not a child. I am twenty years old, I've been on my own since seventeen years of age. If there's something I need to know, I want to know what it is!* It seemed like they were afraid to be honest with me about my future. At that time, I didn't know what was going to happen to me—if I would ever go home, or to an institution, or back to heaven with Nana.

Thoughts of Nana, our neighbor, Mr. Z., and all the long past relatives Nana had introduced me to whirled through my mind. Dad had told me about the condition I was in when he first arrived at General Hospital on that fateful Memorial Day evening: grim, to say the least. The attending doctors were giving my parents half-hour updates regarding my condition, and no one expected me to live through that night. Dad also told me that I had suffered three close head injuries and of my being submerged in water for close to twenty minutes. The prognosis of being "normal" was a stretch, and he was told to expect the worst, permanent brain injury. I had drowned, and no vital signs were present when I was first extracted from the stream. It appeared, upon the initial inspection of the vehicle, that I, too, had gone through the windshield. The EMT personnel who first responded to the accident and arrived at the scene had told my Dad that it was an absolute miracle that I had resuscitated. It is estimated that my lung function was at 25 percent for both lungs combined.

The days that followed were pretty much the same. Mom, Dad, and my baby brother came and went. Some friends stopped by, but not as often as I would have liked. Eventually, visits from friends dwindled from few and far between to non-existent. Even Becki was too busy to come. I guess the novelty of being in the hospital and visiting me had then become a burden to everyone.

My dreams and thoughts were full of Nana. I wanted to be on our rock and ask her the zillions of questions that had formulated in my mind about *what now?* On one of my many hallway jaunts, I stopped by the nurses' station and asked one of the nurses if there was a Catholic priest there that day. I asked if he could stop by my room. I had about an hour to kill before he came. Many questions were swirling in my mind that I wanted answers to about my experience of life on the other side. I was hoping he could explain why I had experienced life on the other side and had come back.

He brought a communion, a prayer book, and a big smile. He was an average-sized, middle-aged gentleman who was a little chubby, wore black horn-rimmed glasses, had thinning black hair, and was a very nice man. He was wearing his black suit with a white collar around his neck. He smelled like peppermint. He asked me if I had anything particular on my mind. I told him about being with Nana. After I finished my saga, he looked at me like a cow looks at a new fence, totally blank. He cleared his throat and said, "Well, Darlene, you've been through a terrible ordeal. Sometimes when that happens the mind plays tricks on you for survival. It's quite possible it was all a dream. A very *real* dream for you, but nonetheless a dream. You received some very heavy-duty medication after you were admitted. All that combined with three closed head injuries, so it's no wonder this dream seems like a reality to you. My advice to you is to continue with following the doctor's orders, get plenty of rest, and don't worry about it—you'll be fine. Eventually, your mind will clear and things will resume to normal for you."

Well, that turned me upside down and paddled me blue! A man of "faith," a man "of the cloth," a man whose only job is to help people develop their spiritual growth was telling me it was all in my head! That scripture verse I once heard at Mass, "Walk by faith and not by sight" (2 Corinthians 5:7) or, in the Lord's Prayer, the verse that says, "On earth, as it is in heaven" … hadn't he ever read or pondered those verses before? Didn't he even just once stop to think about the implication of those verses? That we as a human race need to first acknowledge that life after death is a reality? He didn't believe me.

He didn't believe it truly happened! *That's it. I'm a nut job.* I was evidently not someone who is important or influential enough to have a near death experience. After all, I was living in sin with Tom, and I drank *way* too much alcohol. Plus, I'd been doing $120 a day of cocaine and speed for many weeks before the car accident. I had been on mind-altering medication while in the hospital.

I saw it all in perspective. I was a bona fide nut job. I would have probably started talking to my shoes next. Oh, boy! I was a complete emotional mess. I was sad. I was scared and lonely. I wanted to be with Nana so badly. My parents and Tom were feuding over me. What else could have happened? Although the visits from my friends had stopped, Becki called me regularly. All sorts of negative attitudes and comments were being dumped on me about Tom, by *everyone*. Were the IVs in my arms invisible? Did I look like I could handle this? I was still in the hospital, for God's sake! Couldn't all of you have just shut up and waited until I was stronger and out of the hospital before telling me I had to make a decision about *my* future with Tom? Did *anyone* really give a shit? I didn't think so. I felt stuck and helpless.

Dr. Manning entered my room on day seven of my second hospital stay extension. He felt I should stay five more days. The lung infection was almost gone using these antibiotics. I had hoped for more peace and quiet from everyone about my future plans, which didn't seem to include me and my wishes!

The next five days rolled by. I started to dread going home. A few weeks earlier it was decided that I should move back with my parents to recuperate. Dr. Manning told me I would not be able to return to work for at least twelve months, if ever. My lungs were too weak to walk on my feet twelve to fourteen hours a day. I had been a bartender at a restaurant in town before the accident. I could not be around that much cigarette smoke. It would kill me. Tom lost his job after the accident, too. In light of the fact that he too was involved in that serious car accident, he had sustained injuries that prevented him from going back to work for a few weeks. He wasn't physically able to do his job in the paper mill and was let go. We wouldn't have been able to afford our apartment with both of us jobless. Besides contemplating my own sanity, I now had to move back home and live with my parents. Parents who hated Tom. Parents who disapproved of my lifestyle and the man I wanted to spend the rest of my life with. Parents who would be a challenge to coexist with peacefully. If I wasn't nuts already, I was positive that I *would* be before this twelve-month sentence was up! "Nana! Come get me!"

Dr. Manning came in on day five to tell me I could go home. The infection in my lungs had cleared up, but they were severely damaged. I might have had the equivalent of one-quarter of one lung function between the two. And the journey continued.

Chapter 6

BACK TO EMOTIONAL REALITY

Darlene

The day of going home came on July 18, 1978. My stay in General Hospital was over. Mom needed to dig through my old clothes to find jeans small enough for me to wear home. I weighed in at 92 pounds. Dad treated us all to lunch at the A&W before we went home. We arrived at the house and climbed the stairs. This was the beginning of my "new" life.

For the first few months, things progressed as well as could be expected. Recuperating and Tom were my only concerns. My parents were not thrilled in the least to find that I was *not* going to stop seeing and being in love with Tom. My parents would continually speak of Tom in negative and ugly terms, wanting me to "kick him to the curb," saying "He's no good," and asking "Really, what *do* you *see* in this boy?" I would not listen to them. It didn't matter to me what they thought. It was *my life*. I was twenty years old. I could handle it. They blamed Tom for the entire accident. That was completely unfair, because *I* was the one who talked him into going out for a day of Memorial Day drinking to a party in Vermont.

Tom and I would talk about the car crash, and he would seemingly not want to speak of my "experience" when our conversations would turn to my being outside of this world's realm. Tom's mother, Francis, was half-blooded Cherokee Indian from the Northwest United States. She birthed Tom Kinson, Jr. on Mother's Day, May 14, 1957, on one of the Cherokee reservations in Yakima, Washington. She was very in tune with spiritual intuition. I had mentioned one time to Mama K., Tom's mother, about my out of body experience, and she was pretty much the only one who believed me. She related to me that her own mother had had a similar experience during her young adult life. Unfortunately, I was never able to speak with her about it in-depth before she passed.

At the end of summer, I found myself enrolled at the Vo-Tech College, located on the outskirts of our town. I studied Secretarial Science, taking a one-year diploma course. I graduated in June of 1979 and began my first real job as a secretary at the Coca-Cola plant office. I could—and did—walk to work from our first two-bedroom apartment on Main Street, which was just up the street. At that point, I was newly pregnant with our daughter, Jessica Kate. She was a miracle baby because of all the internal injuries I had sustained from the car crash. When I was released from the hospital, I was told that I would probably never be able to conceive. Medical books were updated again. I was pregnant, and Tom and I were overjoyed about it. I never experienced any of the problems that I was well-versed in from my doctor that could or would happen to my body as a result of the pregnancy. This was surprising, considering my body was still in poor condition from the car wreck. Tom and I were living together again. He was working as much as he could. His mother, Francis Kinson, was our on-call babysitter. I say on-call because she would call and ask if we would like to go out for awhile; she was more than happy to babysit. When Granny K. was there, Jessica never saw her bed.

One morning we got a call from the General Hospital in our little town. It was Tom's father. Tom's mom had passed away due to complications from having viral pneumonia. The night before she passed, I had called her at the hospital. She was speaking of "going home," and saying "I'm just too tired to do this anymore," "Take care of Tom and my baby granddaughter," "I love you like my own daughter." She knew she would be leaving us all. Tom had a very special bond with his mother. He took her death very hard. He started drinking very heavily, and he was starting to be physically abusive with me as a result of his being intoxicated all the time. I just wouldn't allow that.

We ended up splitting up for close to a year. I moved back home with my parents. Again. Jessica was three-and-a-half months old when our split happened. It was very difficult for me to be home again with my infant daughter, living at my parents' home. I would keep asking God, "Why?" Was this the *much work* Nana had spoken of before I left her? I didn't know what was becoming of my life. This wasn't the plan—to be a single mother.

To say Becki and I are vastly different in our life point of views is an understatement! I have always had my feet on the ground and not always looking for pie-in-the-sky solutions. Not that Becki was, but we have always had vastly different attitudes about life in general. My parents raised us kids to think for ourselves and not to be influenced by others' opinions—to gather the facts, as ugly as they were, then make a choice. I'm a realist; I know my position, and I respect others' positions. That being said, I have never allowed myself to be dominated ... *ever!* This is probably why, at this stage of my game, I'm not overly compassionate when others choose their own destinies. Meaning, if one wants to go with what's popular, I'm on the sidelines. I don't support anything without doing my homework first, per se.

When I realized for the first time what it meant to really believe and accept Jesus Christ as my Lord and Savior, I did. I didn't want to take the chance that I would not be allowed back in where I met and walked with my Nana. I wanted to do this *right now.* After the accident when I was home, I started going back to church faithfully. I went back to my roots—the Catholic Church. However, I felt incomplete with that. We, as a congregation, were never instructed to read the Bible. In fact, the complete opposite was taught. We were to trust that the priests would interpret the Bible for us and teach us from the pulpit because that's just the way it was. The priests were the only ones who were called to interpret the Bible and would understand and deliver its teachings to the congregation. The Bible was not something the general population of the Catholic Church was encouraged to read for themselves, by themselves. This didn't feel right to me. When a friend of mine—someone who had attended the Vo-Tech at the same time I did and who also belonged to the Catholic Church—started attending a full Gospel church and asked me to visit her new church, I went. In all the years of my Catholic upbringing, I had never been told I needed to personally accept Jesus Christ as my savior to avow it. In this church, everyone had a Bible and actually read it for himself or herself! What a concept! When I was given a Bible to look things up on my own, I did! I searched out the recesses of my soul. I'm not perfect by any stretch of the imagination, but my belief system was grounded on facts and faith. One cannot possibly be spiritual without knowing the Spirit. One is sorely fooling oneself if one thinks it's possible to have the answers without gaining the knowledge from the spirit of God and his universe.

This has been my quest: to understand spiritual and universal laws. I was raised as a Roman Catholic. This was not a bad thing; however, I did not know anything about the Spirit. I knew rules and regulations. Now, it's a new day. I do know the Spirit, I do know when things are not good, and I do have a mind. And I do use my voice, as unpopular as it is! I will never fault anyone for his or her beliefs; everyone has that choice. But when I know that I know that I know, ya can't shut me up!

My Nana once told me that all that glitters is not gold. She's right. I cannot explain how I know things; it's a deep-seeded thing in my core being. It will not let me rest until I come to terms with it. Meaning, I have to choose. God said that he sets right and wrong before us. He would that we choose right, but again it's our choice. Have I always chosen right? Hell, *no!* And I've paid the price for choosing the wrong things. I chose to ignore the still small voice in my core. And getting back on track took me around Robin Hood's barn. And yet, when I finally agreed to let go and let God ... he still loves me! This is the realization that has delivered me from myself on numerous occasions. Did I want friends? Yes. Did I want to be accepted? Yes. Did I have plenty of both? No. I'm in good company.

So, when we—Tom, myself, and our daughter, Jessica—got involved with a church, we were there in every sense of the word. It was a new beginning. I remember telling Becki about our newfound faith, and she was convinced I'd been suckered into a cult! She wasn't about to jump on that bandwagon. She couldn't grasp the spiritual rebirth I was experiencing. To her, it sounded like I was being brainwashed, and she was worried about me. It put a wedge in our friendship, too. Was it the right place to be for me? At that time, yes. But when you rely on the spirit of God to direct you, you find yourself in a lot of different places. And you're not always in the same place for too long. Core knowing will keep you alert to change and timing. Again, I've not always been on board with this. Many, many times I've been seriously pissed off at God.

When our miracle child, Jessica, was taken away at the age of nineteen in a car accident on October 6, 1999, I was pissed at God for years! If anyone would tell me that this was God's plan, I would have had to restrain myself from punching them dead in the face. How could this be part of God's plan? It was. That stark reality is evermore. I recall on a rainy Saturday afternoon, I was sitting with Jessica at the table and coloring. She was nine years old at the time. We had been coloring for a little while when Jessica stopped, put down her crayons, folded her hands on the table, and said to me, "Mom? My angel sat on my bed last night, and she told me I will not live long enough to have babies." I was so taken back by this statement that I didn't know how to respond. She continued, "It's okay, though." If she had produced a 2x4 from underneath the kitchen table and smacked me on the head with it, I wouldn't have been more shaken. What does a mother say to a statement like that? It was like she was trying to prepare me for her own death. There were more than a few times when she was a very small child that she would tell me her angel had sat on her bed and read her stories from a large brown book. I asked her what the stories were about, but she couldn't remember them. She would always say her angel was beautiful and that she smelled nice—like cotton candy.

When Tom received a job promotion and Jessica was about sixteen years old, we moved to Maine and rented a wonderful three-bedroom ranch style home with a beautiful in-ground pool in the backyard. Beyond that, there was another backyard that was overgrown and lay adjacent to the perimeter of a state wildlife sanctuary. We cleared that area to enjoy a horseshoe pit and garden. Many times living there, we were privileged to see the array of wildlife that lived there. They would wander about our garden and feast upon it. Deer and moose were our most frequent visitors.

On one warm and sunny fall day, Jessica and I were sitting on the deck and she was 19 then. We both had the day off from our prospective jobs. We spent our time visiting and laughing, completely enjoying our time together and the weather. We could find the silliest things to let our imaginations go and laugh ourselves to a tizzy! We were at a lull in our conversation and were just sitting and watching the breezes blow through the tall trees around the edge of backyard. Jessica turned to look at me and said, "Mom, I'm not going to live to see my twentieth birthday. I'm going to die in a car accident."

I almost fell out of my chair! Immediately my mind went back to the time when she was nine and had told me she wasn't going to live long enough to have babies. I did not want to believe this! How could she have known?

It was exactly three weeks from that day that a local policeman was at our door at 5 a.m. and told us we needed to call a detective in Massachusetts and speak to him. Tom called the detective immediately. It was at this time we found out that the car that was registered to the girl who was living with us had been involved in a fatal accident at 11:58 p.m. on I-95 North, just thirty miles south of the Maine border. They had gone to Boston to go clubbing. Two of the girls were dead, and one survived. My immediate thought was *This can't be true*. The driver of the car was the lone survivor and was the girl who was living with us. It took us several hours to figure out which morgue to go to. Jessica was laying there, and there were no IDs to identify the girls. The car accident happened just three weeks to the day after Jessica told us she wasn't going to be with us, just twelve weeks before her twentieth birthday. Jessica had had a divine intuition about her own death. Do I want others to be blessed by my account with the afterlife? Yes. Do I want to prevent others from making *faux pas?* Yes! Can I do it for them? *No!* Again, here is what can happen when you make poor choices and don't listen to your inner being.

To speak honestly, I'm not always in tune with the Spirit. I make dumb-ass choices, because it is easier than getting on my knees and asking for direction. With my intuition, I've experienced knowing places, layouts of the land, and how a house will look inside. I know I've been there before. Another life? Anything is probable. I suppose what I've gleaned from my personal experience with the other side, is this: when you stop breathing, it doesn't mean death. Sometimes it's a wakeup call. It was for me. However, the opinions of others "in the know" semi- convinced me that I hadn't really had that experience in heaven.

I had my parents, doctors, clergymen, and friends who told me my experience was a drug-induced thing. Sorry. It wasn't. Becki had given me a book called *Proof of Heaven*. In this book he details about his own near death experience as a result of a near fatal rare brain illness. He explains how when a person is in a coma, his or her brain ceases to function. During that state of a non-functioning brain, there is no traceable sign of activity within the brain that would allow any kind of monitoring, measuring, or reaction to what you are experiencing. There is no way any signal is received when this happens, as when dreaming or hallucinating. He concludes that near death experiences are real. And I know *my* experience was real! Why me? I have no clue. Will anyone take me seriously? I have no clue.

Will it change anything for anybody? I have no clue. I'm just stating my facts.

At a Wednesday night church service one time, I was at the altar on my knees, practically begging Jesus to talk to me personally. I remember saying to him, "I know I was there. Why didn't I see you?" The response took me back. The small, still voice in my spirit said, "Because when I look at sin, I have to judge it." So, even if I'd been allowed to stay with Nana, I wouldn't have stayed. How do I know this? It's in his, God's, book. I was far from being an obedient child! I was spouting that there was no God. I was living a lifestyle in direct opposition to the will of God. I was a brat! Does this new enlightenment mean that I'm without flaw? Of course not! I still make hasty decisions when I should pray and receive guidance. I still have anger issues that I'm learning to deal with and overcome. I still do not always choose the right way. Does it mean God has cast me aside? No. I've cast him aside with my own decisions. And, in my own experiences, that's a very lonely place to be.

My BFF, Becki, recently gave me another book to read by Marc Allen, about the spiritual awakening sweeping across America now and the "simple steps to abundance, fulfillment, and a life well lived." I realized that his book is pretty much an interpretation, in a simple form, of God's word—the Bible. God's word promises abundance, health, fulfillment, and joy overflowing! I've read and reread these promises from God's word, and I believe them. But in recent years, I've neglected them for myself. Do I expect them? Yes. But faith without work is dead. To work oneself into a tizzy for the church will earn no one extra "points," and I'm not saying getting involved with a purpose isn't a good thing; I'm saying that sometimes we get caught up with doing things and we overextend ourselves physically and neglect our spiritual growth. Growth in the spirit is much like growth in our physical bodies; we need sleep to grow. Not laziness, but quiet time. Time to allow meditation. Time to pray. Time to be by yourself without the distractions of being there for someone else and their needs. Time to be prepared for the manifestation of that which we desire in our own life experience. It's not a spiritual competition; it takes reflection and evaluation of yourself for those things that you most desire. It takes a readiness to not be understood by your family and friends. Believe me, they will get in your face about your new approach to your own happiness! I believe this is the work that Nana told me I needed to do. It's not once-and-for-all work; it's an everyday sifting and sorting of what it is you want in your life. Then, once you know what you want, *believe* you can attain it, and don't kill it with words and thoughts of doubt and disbelief. We are all guilty of that. It takes focus and perseverance, and most of all faith that what you ask for will be given to you. It's time to be selfish about your spiritual growth!

It's been my personal experience with my spiritual growth that when I push the hardest for something I want and I have to have it *now*, I have to wait longer to receive it or it won't manifest at all. The spiritual realm relies only on timing and your own readiness to receive. If you don't see the answers to your desires manifesting then you must still be in doubt about it and your only work is to change your thoughts to believe in them. *No* one else can be a proxy for you; it has to be your own work to focus and believe you can have your desires. So, there you have it.

In the introduction of our book, Becki wrote that she has been experiencing an awakening of her spirit to universal truths and manifestations and that she has been implementing and using our angels to bring messages and life questions to heaven—and that the answers are brought back to us. Well, *yeah!* If anyone is a believer of

God's word, it's his promise to us. All we have to do is line ourselves up with his spiritual laws. However, we (human beings) are not always willing to "let go and let God" direct us. Most often we want the bounty of all his promises but refuse to change what needs to be changed for the manifestations to take place. Doubt and worry are the biggest abundant-life suckers for us all. We are not to fret and worry about the things we ask guidance for. All things are possible with God. It's been my personal experience that when God wants me to make a change in my spiritual life, I kick, holler, and scream like a spoiled rotten brat! It's not God who leaves; it's *me* who dictates my timeline, and my timeline is not God's. I get on my horse of self-righteousness and have a tendency at times to be judgmental of others, to think the worst of people without reason—and to not show compassion toward others or maintain a spirit of gratitude and thankfulness. These are biggies for me. My husband Tom will remind me now and again when I'm in the mode of *stinkin' thinkin',* a phrase we use with each other when either of us falls into ungratefulness or not being thankful. So, with that being said, I read the books she gives me and continue to read my Bible. Although we, Tom and me, have not attended a traditional church building in awhile, the truths of the spirit are very much acknowledged in both my husband's life and mine on a daily basis. To wake up each morning is God's grace to "get it right." It's the *do over* I ask for all the time.

I was born, baptized, schooled, and actively participated in the Roman Catholic faith until I was thirty-two years old. I remember attending Mass one Sunday morning and I felt absolutely empty of any spiritualism in my life. It scared me! Why did I feel so void? I had no answers. I'd seen a friend at Mass over the previous months and then noticed she wasn't attending Mass anymore. I picked up the phone and called her to see if everything was okay with her. She assured me that everything was great! She began telling me about a different church she had begun attending where they actually *read* the Bible and where the praise and worship music was exhilarating! What? Reading the Bible for yourself and actually enjoying the songs sung in church? Unfathomable! I decided to visit her "new" church, the Assembly of God, with my daughter, Jessica, one Sunday morning and that was that. The pastor addressed all the life questions, difficulties, and emptiness I had been experiencing in my private life. I was miffed at my friend, as I thought she had told him I would be visiting that church that Sunday and that she had given him some information about my life—thus, the sermon that day. She told me that she hadn't said a word to the pastor about my being there that Sunday and that if God chose to use him to address my life, then that's God.

The first thing I had to retrain myself with was my general conception of the spiritual realm. I believed there was God, Jesus Christ, and the Holy Spirit. I believed that angels and saints were also part of the spiritual realm; however, to communicate with them—to ask for divine intervention from them—was not their forte. How incorrect I was in that line of thinking! The reality of angels and saints is that they are our personal advisors. Their purpose in our own spiritual life is to be our backup. They are our link to the spiritual laws that govern *all* things. Saints in particular are our allies in this "real" world. The accounts of their lives are to validate our own uniqueness as human beings. They were not without flaws. Growth, for the most part, cannot happen until a mistake or mess happens. At least that is the case with myself. How many times have I retained an attitude or concept that was totally off the mark?

Our initial concepts of life are instilled in us by people who are in the positions of teachers, role models, and family. Let's get real here for a minute; most of my own concepts of life were witnessed by the people in direct contact with me. I'm not saying that everything I was taught were wrong— and far from it. It's only that some of those attitudes or beliefs were meant for them and their circumstances and were not specifically for me. When confusion was all I had, as I've come to know, it was because the situations of my life, at that time, were completely different from those of people who influenced me. It's like the old saying, "Ya can't talk the talk unless you've walked the walk."

People are sometimes put into our lives to show us where our own thinking or perceptions need an adjustment. Sometimes their lives are our "map" to getting to where we need to be or the next rung we need to step up on in order to make needed changes or to test ourselves. As I said earlier, Becki and I have vast differences in our attitudes about things and the workings of this life. That doesn't mean that we're wrong; it means that what might fit for one of us won't necessarily fit for the other.

After I came out of the car accident, my whole perception of life was different. Life is fragile. Life, as we know it, can and will change in the blink of an eye. Things are not usually what we think they should be. Case in point: I was told by well-educated medical personnel that I would never be able to conceive because of the internal injuries I sustained as a result of that accident. Ten months after the accident, I was pregnant! Jessica Kate Kinson was living prove of that. She was our miracle baby.

Chapter 7

LIFE CONTINUES AFTER THE CRASH

Becki

Years passed since the crash, and our lives flowed together and apart like huge waves in the ocean. After Darlene came home from the hospital, our partying days were over. We started our families and settled down into adulthood with responsibilities that go with raising a family. Little did we know we had more bumps in the road ahead. Darlene and I were always in sync with our core rhythms. For example, we were pregnant with our first child at the same time. Our lives were so closely in sync that when I was leaving the hospital on January 6, 1980 after having my son Tom on the 3rd, Darlene came in the door the same day I left to give birth to Jessica Kate that night. She took the same bed in the maternity ward that I had occupied, and Jessica occupied the same bed in the nursery as Tom had just hours earlier! Becki's Tommy was the first baby born that year in our local hospital. You can't make it up! The two were playmates for years. Darlene and I are both lefties, and we always tend to finish each other's thoughts quite easily, as we noticed when we were writing this book.

Darlene and Tom raised their beautiful little girl, Jessica Kate, in our little hometown—with her azure blue eyes and strawberry-blond curly hair. Most of Jessica's schooling was spent at christian schools, between Calvary Baptist School and another area christian school. We both raised our children in the Christian religion as our parents and ancestors had in the past. We thought it was the thing to do as part of being "good parents." I had three beautiful, handsome boys with my first husband—Thomas, Nickolas, and Adam.

Darlene and I always stayed in touch, making play dates, and in our twenties we never went very long without contact. We lived close by and knew we were always there if either of us needed something, including mental support. Darlene and Tom stayed together through thick and thin, and I went through a stressful divorce after seven years of marriage, becoming a single mother of three in 1986. I was in desperate times mentally and financially and had to move in with my mother for awhile. I reunited with an old flame from high school that didn't work out, but we had a beautiful daughter, Aimee. I ended up alone again, raising my kids by myself. This was a very trying time in my life. I didn't know my purpose or how to get myself out of this hole I was in. Darlene was very supportive. I thank God I had her. She helped me with babysitting and keeping my head straight. It was in 1989 that I met my life partner, Jim. He was so handsome—with dark hair and blue eyes. I was in love and knew he was perfect! We had our hard times, as he had three kids too, but we managed to stay together. He eventually became my second husband in 2005.

I got a call one day in October of 1998—one that I never wanted to receive—that Jessica Kate had lost her life in a car crash in Massachusetts. *No, this is not for real!* I thought. *This can't happen to my best friend! She has had enough tragedy in this life.* Darlene, Tom, and Jessica were living in Maine at the time of Jessica's death. I was in New Hampshire. I immediately went to Darlene's parents' house in our hometown to provide support and grieve her loss with her. What do you say? This just wasn't supposed to happen to us. Darlene was all doped up on drugs her Dad made sure she had, per her doctor's orders. I still think the reason she had such a hard time with life afterward was that she didn't get a chance to grieve. Tom was naturally a mess as well. It was definitely a week from hell; I just didn't know how to handle it. There was nothing I could do to bring her back. This was life-changing enough to depress Darlene for several years after. She was unable to work and get on with life for more than ten years. Simple things—such as hearing music on the radio, watching her favorite shows, or seeing friends—would trigger fond memories that would flood back and be too much for her to bear. Jessica had been her only child, an angel from God. All Darlene wanted was children and grandchildren. I tried to be supportive, but it seemed like I felt so guilty. I had four healthy kids, and it just wasn't fair!

We drifted apart, and as Darlene sank into a deeper depression, eventually on several mixes of medications, I was at a loss for what to do. I wished I could just make it all better. We reconnected and met a few times in the years after Jessica died in 1999, but we lost contact with each other after Jim and I moved to North Carolina in 2006 when our kids graduated from high school. We wanted a warmer climate and a change. I was becoming more and more aware of my need to find my purpose and asking for divine guidance through prayer and meditation. Teachers began showing up as the internet was growing in the late 2000s, and I learned about the book *The*

Secret as well as many other books and spiritual authors, with Dr. Wayne Dyer being one of my most important ones.

I didn't even know where Darlene lived! She hadn't shown up at any of our class reunions since our tenth one. It wasn't like her. I was worried something had happened. I didn't run into her until my Dad passed in 2009, when I saw her briefly. I found out she had moved back from Maine to our hometown in New Hampshire, into her mom's apartment downstairs. When my mom fell and broke her hip, I was forced to leave North Carolina and come back to New Hampshire to be closer and care for her.

Darlene and I reconnected, and it was like we had never lost each other. Our souls were the same as they had been before, connected as always. I was beginning to believe Darlene's crazy stories about her past life experience, her visions, and her intuitions. After moving back home, I became obsessed with my own spiritual awakening.

Working in a nursing home in New Hampshire after moving back, an elderly gentleman—a retired doctor in ophthalmology who was in his nineties—had a book sitting on his bedside table, *Conversations with God* by Neale Donald Walsh. He told me he thought of it as his Bible and asked me if I wanted to read it. Of course I was interested; it looked wonderful. I did read it, and my husband did as well. I then was so obsessed that I bought all the rest of his books and found them very enlightening, because it was obvious the words in them came from the divine. There was no way a human being could produce a book with such divine knowledge.

I continued to find the spiritual teachers when I asked. When my cousin's son passed at age twenty-seven in a motorcycle crash, his mother was seeing a psychic medium and having good readings, validating that he was ok. I wanted to experience this with deceased members of my own family, especially my dad and my grandmother. My dad had passed a couple of years before my first psychic reading at my house. The medium showed up at my door, and I was sweating. I was a little scared and skeptical with my daughter attending and my cousin Jill.

The medium was a middle-aged woman, a tiny, pretty lady, whom I knew was Catholic and was well-known. She announced that a father figure and a woman named Jane was with her all the way to my house, wanting to connect with me. I was blown away at the reading when my dad came through by singing his favorite church hymn from his funeral, "The Old Rugged Cross." It was one of his favorite hymns, and my stepmother validated it by exclaiming "He sang it all the time!"

Jane was a friend and coworker whom I met in North Carolina; she had passed the year before and told me that she was okay. She wanted me to know I had been a good friend and that she had enjoyed working with me. I was in tears. My dad told me he loved me, because he rarely said it enough when he was alive and wanted to be sure I knew. It was a life-changing hour for me. Even my dog Teddy came through, describing him to a T. More relatives came through with messages for me, and my daughter Aimee had a good experience as well with other family members. After that, I wanted more. I went to every event the medium presented that came up periodically, and I brought my friends along—always hearing from my dad. My grandmother, who hadn't come through until recently, when the book was in the works, told me she was helping me write it and was very supportive. How would the medium know that? Nobody knew we were writing a book at that time. Darlene's grandmother, Nana, who came through with her name Mildred, told me that not all that glitters is gold, and she was talking about the book. I never figured that out until a couple of months later when I was reading the book and discovered that Darlene had written that her Nana (Mildred) said that right in the book. You can't make it up!

I was seeking my life purpose, and I couldn't get enough answers from the teachers. I found them on my favorite spiritual radio station, through books, and on Facebook. I would type in *angels, meditations,* or *healthy lifestyles* and receive so much information. I soaked up, pondered, and learned from inspirational people, events, and groups that seemed to never end. I found how to connect with my angels and guides through card readings and learned to do it myself from famous spiritualists. I learned how to listen to my guides about synchronicity, about the difference between spirit and religion. I know I don't believe in many of my old teachings of the Bible; I am learning that the universe/God is all one entity, and we are all connected. We vibrate at different frequencies and bounce off each other in the physical, like a dance. I also know that I can change my reality by changing my thoughts. I can follow the path of least resistance. My life has improved with every new change I have made. Good things come easily to me: the comfortable homes I find to rent and own, my perfect job as an occupational therapist, working for the visiting nurses. I am a new author and writer. I'm learning to paint beautiful pictures, like the one I did on the cover of this book (with a little help). It just keeps getting better all the time. My point is that my spiritual awakening has changed my life. When I think about my best friend, Darlene—who has been trying to tell me the truth about what happened when her spirit left her body that day after the crash—I really believe that her visit to heaven was *real*.

I talked Darlene into coming to my house for a psychic reading on March 30, 2014, because I truly believed she would benefit hearing from her daughter Jessica and her nana. It was ironic that when the day of the reading came, her father did pass from Alzheimer's that early morning at 4:00 a.m. The reading was planned for 6 p.m. that evening, and Darlene still wanted to come. She knew he was going to pass soon from Alzheimer's, as he was seeing Jessica Kate—his first granddaughter and Darlene's only daughter—who had passed on October 6, 1999. The same medium was there that had come before. She had never met Darlene, and right off the bat Darlene got the first reading. The medium reported that Darlene's dad, Leon, was with her all the way there, pushing everyone else aside. The medium didn't believe he had just passed that day, as it was unusual for a soul to come through in such a short amount of time after passing—less than fourteen hours earlier. Jessica was with him during the reading, and that was comforting. He brought up so much that nobody but Darlene would know. We cried and laughed at the humor he brought! He was always a practical joker. The evening passed quickly.

Everyone had a great experience and validation that their loved ones on the other side were fine and happy. All seven of us heard from our loved ones during the reading. It was a success. Most who had come were skeptical, but not after that day. My dad came through for me, and for my stepmother, Claire, who had lost her son years earlier, also at a young age. We all felt so good afterward, knowing they were okay and had so many messages for us. They were described perfectly, and Darlene couldn't wrap her head around it. It was a relief to have healing begin. I felt it was a big release that had finally occurred for her that night. She knew her father had passed earlier that morning but had chosen not to tell me because she really thought this was a bunch of whoo-ha and wanted to rub my nose in it! How wrong she was! This brought us even closer to spirit, and that was when I kept getting the message from my angels and guides that I needed to write this book! We've learned through our spiritual teachings that signs of angels and divine guidance come through intuitions—just knowing or feeling strongly about something you need or want to do. Finding feathers, or coins, or seeing images in the clouds and colorful orbs in pictures are common signs that spirit is with us. Believe me; we get them.

Darlene and Tom moved to Florida on June 14, shortly after her dad passed in 2014. Jim and I were back in our hometown in New Hampshire to be near my ninety-one-year old mom with ataxia disease that has crippled her to the point of being unable to walk. Grandkids were multiplying. As I said in the introduction about how this book came to be, an inspiration came to me in the middle of the night when my spirit guides told me, "You need to tell this story, because it's true from our hearts." When Darlene and I agreed to get this book going, we worked on it from 1,600 miles apart until it became impossible to write from such a long distance away. Jim and I made a quick visit in March 2015 to exchange some of the content, but after doing the bulk on our own, chatting, and e-mailing, we found we had to meet a few more times to finish this together, since Darlene's memories kept flooding back, more and more.

I went to Florida in the summer of 2015 for a week on vacation alone and to cocreate this divine book with the events of Memorial Day on May 28, 1978. Staying with Darlene and Tom in their condo on the beach was like being in heaven. It was truly meant to be. We took walks on the beach and found our millions of feathers that she exclaimed were normally scarce—until I arrived. The beach was layered with them. We swam and wrote for five days straight. Darlene's husband Tom, was fondly known as the *kitchen bitch* (as he called himself). All joking aside, he kept us with meals and drinks throughout the day. He was a trooper!

On one of our nightly walks down the beach, two girls were standing there holding a small baby turtle that was all black with yellow spots. They said it had been floating up on the beach in the waves and they picked it up. It seemed to be still alive—just barely. We immediately took it, as we had a permanent home on the beach to go to and Darlene wanted to try to save it. When we got back to the condo, we put him in a bowl with water and lettuce, picked hay for his bed, and set out to find out more about him. We looked up his color and details on the internet to find out that he wasn't even a species from Florida! We called the marine turtle hospital, and they reported that they had never heard of this kind of turtle. He wasn't a water turtle, for sure. He was a three-inch long baby leopard land tortoise, not a turtle at all. He came from Africa and was banned from America in 2000 due to health problems. We called a turtle rescue organization to find out that they wouldn't take him and that he would have to be eliminated for that reason. There was no way we were going to give him to anyone at that point! He was ours and was so adorable. We pampered him for three days and tried to feed him and hold him, but he wasn't moving very much. He ate very little, and the day before I left, he passed away. Darlene and I were so sad. Why had we been blessed with this little fella—not a sea turtle but a land turtle found floating in the ocean and drowning? Darlene and I were used to having divine messages sent to us, and we would answer each other's thoughts as if we had the same mindset, especially while writing our book. After that, we saw turtles in every cloud we saw. He was telling us he was okay in heaven. We named him D-Tony after Daytona. The message coming from this baby tortoise was, we believe: "Don't allow yourself to get washed up on the beach. Stay strong, allow yourself to receive help, and never give up."

He knew he wasn't wanted here, and he went back to tortoise heaven. We will never forget him. Now we see turtles everywhere—in gift shops and in the clouds.

Chapter 8

OUR DIVINE REALIZATIONS

This divine manuscript has given us the realization that by changing your thoughts and beliefs, you can change your life for the greatest and highest good—because once you change your thoughts (good or bad), the manifestation happens. We proved it! Here's how we did it.

The first thought that came to Becki was to tell Darlene that she needed to tell her story for many reasons. Becki had believed her story for the past few years, but it wasn't until this became a huge wave of energy—consumed by divine guidance and the realization that she was unable to let it go—that it was done! Darlene was very resistant to Becki's "realization" and the thought that anyone would believe or be interested in her life after her near death experience. So, Becki being fully convinced and *believing* in the divine inspiration to write this book, continued to pray for Darlene, hoping that she wound receive this inspiration too and change her thoughts of doubt and disbelief. Spiritual laws are constant—they never lie—and it's only a matter of time before they open one's eyes to the truth and make one believe it for oneself.

Just by changing your thoughts, you can change your life.

Darlene did finally accept the challenge to write the story—and changed her thoughts into believing again that her own near death experience was and is possible, knowing that heaven was real. She also realized that other people would now believe and accept the knowing of her divine experience. This gave Darlene a new opening and outlook on life! It opened the door for the two of us to be on the same spiritual page. We are blessed and grateful.

We proved to ourselves that by changing our thoughts, our divine book has manifested all our hopes and dreams. Our lives have changed forever!

My friendship with Darlene has survived forty-seven years, and counting. I'm happy with our journey—the good and the bad—and the lessons learned continue in life and are the reason we are here. It seems that when we were at difficult lows in our lives, we had to go through them separately—but we were always there for each other. The lows have taught us to be at peace with ourselves and our spirits. We are kindred spirits and always will be. I'm so blessed to have come to believe Darlene's spiritual truths and will never waver again. There is no ending to our story. We will go on with our divine experiences and many more memories to be created. Who knows? Another book might be in the works!

Darlene and Becki
We love you all.
Namaste

Printed in the United States
By Bookmasters